Building SPELLING Skills

Grade 6

Daily Practice

What's in This Book?

This 30-unit book contains strategies and practice for learning 540 spelling words.

Each unit contains:

- a list of 18 spelling words
- two sentences for dictation
- four activity pages for practicing the spelling words

Words on the spelling lists were selected from:

- a list of the 600 most commonly used words in English
- words frequently misspelled by sixth-graders
- words with common phonetic elements
- words changed by adding prefixes and suffixes and by forming compound words and contractions

Additional resources:

- "How to Study" chart
- "Spelling Strategies" chart
- forms for testing and recordkeeping

Correlated **to State Standards**

Visit *www.teaching-standards.com* to view a correlation of this book's activities to your state's standards. This is a free service.

EMC 2710

Evan-Moor®
EDUCATIONAL PUBLISHERS
Helping Children Learn since 1979

Author: Martha Cheney
Editor: Leslie Sorg
Copy Editor: Cathy Harber
Illustrator: Jim Palmer
Desktop: Jia-Fang Eubanks, Yuki Meyer

Congratulations on your purchase of some of the finest teaching materials in the world.

For information about other Evan-Moor products, call 1-800-777-4362, fax 1-800-777-4332, or visit our Web site, www.evan-moor.com.

18 Lower Ragsdale Drive, Monterey, CA 93940-5746. Printed in USA.

Contents

Teaching the Weekly Unit

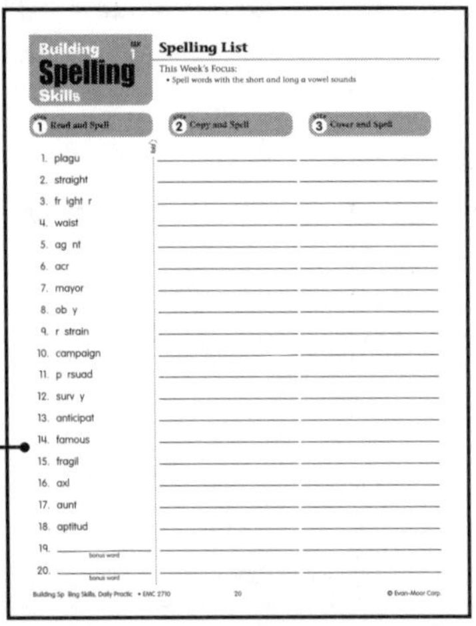
Building Spelling Skills

Spelling List

This Week's Focus:

1 Read and Spell — 2 Copy and Spell — 3 Cover and Spell

1. plagu
2. straight
3. fr ight r
4. waist
5. ag nt
6. acr
7. mayor
8. ob y
9. r strain
10. campaign
11. p rsuad
12. surv y
13. anticipat
14. famous
15. fragil
16. axl
17. aunt
18. aptitud
19. bonus word
20. bonus word

Monday's Page

Strengthening Students' Spelling Skills

Spelling Strategies — Building Spelling Skills

Say a word correctly.
• Don't leave out or mispronounce sounds.
• Write the sounds in the correct order.

Think about what the word looks like.
• Think about how the spelling pattern looks.
• Write it, look at it, and decide if it looks correct.

Look for small words in spelling words.
• spin—pin, in
• cupcake—cup, cake

Look at syllables in spelling words.
• Spell the word one syllable at a time.
remember—re • mem • ber

Use rhyming words to help spell a word.
• If you can spell book, you can spell look.

Use rules for adding endings.
• Drop the silent e before adding a suffix.
• Double the final consonant before adding a suffix.
• Change the final y to i and add es.

Use knowledge of prefixes and suffixes.

How to Study Your List — Building Spelling Skills

1 Read and Spell
2 Copy and Spell
3 Cover and Spell
4 Uncover and Check

Spelling Strategies Page 6

How to Study Your List Page 7

At the beginning of the year, reproduce pages 6 and 7 for each student or on an overhead transparency. Review the general steps and strategies, encouraging students to apply them throughout the year.

Monday

Allot ample class time each Monday for introducing the spelling list and having students complete the first page of the unit.

Introducing the Week's Words

Give each student the spelling list for the week. Here are ways to introduce the words:

- Call attention to important consistencies noted in "This Week's Focus," such as a phonetic or structural element. For example, say: *As we read this week's spelling list, notice that all the words have the same vowel sound.*
- Read each word aloud and have students repeat it.
- Provide a model sentence using the word. Have several students give their own sentences.
- If desired, add "bonus words" based on the needs of your class. These may be high-utility words or words that the class is encountering in curricular studies.

Writing the Words

After introducing the words, have students study and write the words on the first page of the unit, following these steps:

Step 1: Read and Spell
Have students read the word and spell it aloud.

Step 2: Copy and Spell
Tell students to copy the word onto the first blank line and spell it again, touching each letter as it is spoken.

Step 3: Cover and Spell
Have students fold the paper along the fold line to cover the spelling words so that only the last column shows. Then have students write the word from memory.

Step 4: Uncover and Check
Tell students to open the paper and check the spelling. Students should touch each letter of the word as they spell it aloud.

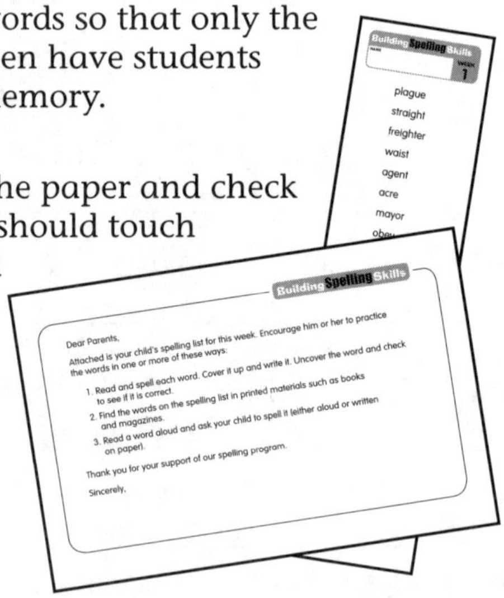
Building Spelling Skills — Week 1

plague
straight
freighter
waist
agent
acre
mayor

Dear Parents,

Attached is your child's spelling list for this week. Encourage him or her to practice the words in one or more of these ways:

1. Read and spell each word. Cover it up and write it. Uncover the word and check to see if it is correct.
2. Find the words on the spelling list in printed materials such as books and magazines.
3. Read a word aloud and ask your child to spell it (either aloud or written on paper).

Thank you for your support of our spelling program.

Sincerely,

Home Connection

Send home a copy of the Parent Letter (page 145) and the Take-Home Spelling List for the week (pages 10–19).

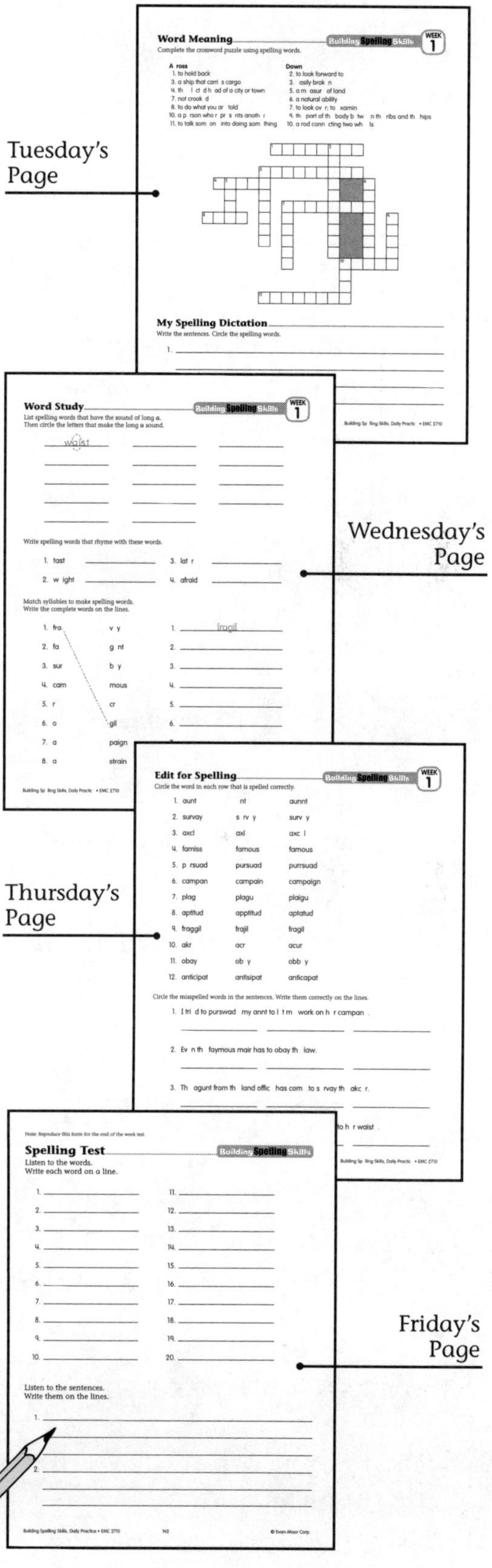

Tuesday — Word Meaning and Dictation

Have students complete the Word Meaning activity on the second page of the unit. Then use the dictation sentences on pages 8 and 9 to guide students through "My Spelling Dictation." Follow these steps:

1. Ask students to listen to the complete sentence as you read it.
2. Say the sentence in phrases, repeating each phrase one time clearly. Have students repeat the phrase.
3. Wait as students write the phrase.
4. When the whole sentence has been written, read it again, having students touch each word as you say it.

Wednesday — Word Study Activities

Have students complete the activities on the third page of the unit. Depending on students' abilities, these activities may be completed as a group or independently.

Thursday — Edit for Spelling Activities

Have students complete the activities on the fourth page. Depending on students' abilities, these activities may be completed as a group or independently.

Friday — Weekly Test

Friday provides students the chance to take the final test and to retake the dictation they did on Tuesday. A reproducible test form is provided on page 142. After the test, students can record their score on the "My Spelling Record" form (page 141).

Spelling Strategies

Say a word correctly.

- Don't leave out or mispronounce sounds.
- Write the sounds in the correct order.

Think about what the word looks like.

- Think about how the spelling pattern looks.
- Write it, look at it, and decide if it looks correct.

Look for small words in spelling words.

- spin—**pin**, **in**
- cupcake—**cup**, **cake**

Look at syllables in spelling words.

- Spell the word one syllable at a time.
  remember—**re • mem • ber**

Use rhyming words to help spell a word.

- If you can spell **book**, you can spell **look**.

Use rules for adding endings.

- Drop the silent **e** before adding a suffix.
- Double the final consonant before adding a suffix.
- Change the final **y** to **i** and add **es**.

Use knowledge of prefixes and suffixes.

- Think about what the word looks like without the prefix or suffix.
- Write the word and then add the prefix or suffix.

How to Study Your List

1 Read and Spell

2 Copy and Spell

3 Cover and Spell

4 Uncover and Check

Sentences for Dictation

There are two dictation sentences for each spelling list. Space for sentence dictation is provided on Tuesday of each week and on Friday's test form (page 142).

- Ask students to listen to the complete sentence as you read it.
- Have students repeat the sentence.
- Read the sentence in phrases, repeating each phrase one time clearly.
- Have students repeat the phrase.
- Allow time for students to write the phrase.
- Read the sentence again, having students touch each word as you say it.

Week	Dictation Sentences
1	The **agent** insisted that the **axle** of the **freighter** be **straight**. My **aunt** has a wonderful **aptitude** for handling **fragile** plants.
2	**Neither** of the **hockey** players **received** penalties for their **illegal** plays. Was the **nominee pleasant** as he spoke about his **achievements**?
3	The **stowaway** was **often** frightened by the **approach** of the **officer**. **Although** the **obstacle** was quite high, the **antelope** was able to jump it.
4	Was the **scientific** community able to **decipher** the origin of the **typhoon**? The wealthy **buyer** wishes to **acquire** the painting this **instant**.
5	The **sculpture** was so **valuable** that it was placed in a **museum**. It is **customary** for kings to **utilize** their wealth to buy **beautiful** art.
6	Do you **recommend** that we form an **alliance** at the earliest **opportunity**? Was Sally **embarrassed** by the **awkward occurrence** at the **barricade**?
7	Mr. Johnson **hesitated** before **gesturing** at the **angriest** man in the crowd. The **loneliest** student **studied** the most and had the **cleanest** room.
8	Did the **absent-minded** pirate forget to bring a **duffel bag** to carry his **outstanding** store of treasures to the island? Do the teachers talk about **themselves** in their **headquarters** at the **high school**?
9	Mrs. Brown's **favorite** students worked **earnestly** to improve their **grammar**. Is the **earthworm worthy** of respect even though it is not **similar** to a human?
10	A **feature** of a seaside vacation is the **pleasure** of feeling the **moisture** in the air. The **catcher** had a **seizure**; he fell and **fractured** his leg.
11	This **ointment** is **efficient enough** without being **oily**. Was the **symphony** thrown into **turmoil** when the conductor began **coughing**?
12	When the **plumber** saw the **gnarled** pipes, he **sighed** and **acknowledged** that it was time to **condemn** the building. The **honorable** knight crossed the **trestle** that led to his enemy's **castle**.
13	Charlie liked the **efficiency** of the **ordinary antenna**. The **article** issued a **warning** about a water **shortage**.

Week	Dictation Sentences
14	**Their insight** was of great **assistance**. **They're all ready** to **censor** the program.
15	That **action** is a **violation** of the law, not a **solution** to the problem. The **musician** sang a song about his **observation** of the **collision**.
16	Try not to **lose** the **patients' stationery**. Our **patience** grew short waiting for the **hostile** fan to **cease** his screaming.
17	Was the tip the **immigrant** gave the **attendant significant**? The **radiant** light from the **brilliant** sun made us all feel **magnificent**.
18	The **official** will **surely** examine the **ashes** to find the cause of the fire. Why was the **magician** so **impatient** to **establish** his show dates?
19	It was **sensible** for him to be **cautious** of the **vicious** driver. Jen gave an **audible** squeal at the sight of the **lovable** puppy and hoped they would be **compatible**.
20	We used **substances** to repel **mosquitoes** while we picked **tomatoes**. Did the **thieves** cross many **boundaries** on their **journeys**?
21	The **government** began a very **successful** road **development** project. The scientist conducted each **experiment** in a **tireless** and **humorless** way.
22	Would it be **inconvenient** to store the **imperfect** items **underneath** your bed? Why was there no **immediate** response to the **uncertain** and **unreliable** report?
23	The Benson brothers **import** and **export graphite**. The **geologist** took the **photograph** with a **portable** camera.
24	My little brother **screamed** and **whined** and **demanded** ice cream. Meg **whispered** when she **answered**, and we **insisted** that she speak louder.
25	I **sincerely** hope there will be a **vacancy** so I can **lengthen** my stay. Was Tim **especially** pleased at his **membership** on the **championship** team?
26	When writing **nonfiction**, you must **rewrite** each word that you **misspell**. The **antisocial nonconformist** seems to **disagree** with everyone.
27	That **ancient** computer is no longer **reliable**, and so it is **obsolete**. We are **optimistic** that no one will be **wasteful** of our **meager** food supply.
28	Did you see the **triathlon** winner flex her **triceps** as she filled out the forms in **triplicate**? Our class sat in a **semicircle** while our **bilingual** teacher taught us about **semicolons**.
29	Each **spectator** watched the volcanic **eruption** through a **telescope**. If you want to show **respect**, don't **interrupt** the woman in the **uniform**.
30	The **cartographer** made a map of a **peninsula** in the Southern **Hemisphere**. Is an **international** team studying the **environment** of **Antarctica**?

Building Spelling Skills

NAME

WEEK 1

plague
straight
freighter
waist
agent
acre
mayor
obey
restrain
campaign
persuade
survey
anticipate
famous
fragile
axle
aunt
aptitude

______ bonus word

______ bonus word

cut

Building Spelling Skills

NAME

WEEK 2

hockey
received
neither
believe
achievement
equality
referee
pleasant
illegal
nominee
electricity
frequent
entry
eagerly
pique
easel
abbreviate
tedious

______ bonus word

______ bonus word

cut

Building Spelling Skills

NAME

WEEK 3

although
moment
goalie
poem
poetry
approach
ceremony
stowaway
trolley
oxygen
often
officer
obstacle
envelope
proverb
antelope
molecule
obstinate

______ bonus word

______ bonus word

Building Spelling Skills

NAME

WEEK 4

buyer
instant
quietly
plight
describe
acquire
typhoon
twice
lithe
scientific
blind
decipher
distinct
xylophone
glimpse
pliable
slight
friction

bonus word

bonus word

cut

Building Spelling Skills

NAME

WEEK 5

country
does
once
beautiful
unusual
unit
fugitive
menu
utilize
sculpture
valuable
thumbprint
museum
universe
luxury
sulfur
customary
suffocate

bonus word

bonus word

cut

Building Spelling Skills

NAME

WEEK 6

occurrence
embarrass
occasion
symmetry
recommend
exaggerate
terrain
barricade
alliance
applaud
hooray
opportunity
opposite
daughter
authentic
awkward
brought
because

bonus word

bonus word

Building Spelling Skills

NAME

WEEK 7

gestured
gesturing
hesitated
hesitating
studied
studying
prescribed
prescribing
skied
skiing
lonelier
loneliest
friendlier
friendliest
cleaner
cleanest
angrier
angriest

bonus word

bonus word

cut

Building Spelling Skills

NAME

WEEK 8

everybody
anywhere
knowledge
brainstorm
stomachache
outstanding
sweatshirt
videotape
meanwhile
old-fashioned
long-distance
duffel bag
child's play
absent-minded
daybreak
high school
headquarters
themselves

bonus word

bonus word

cut

Building Spelling Skills

NAME

WEEK 9

favorite
traitor
circuit
circumvent
rehearse
courtesy
courteous
humor
humorous
energy
energetic
courage
courageous
similar
grammar
worthy
earthworm
earnestly

bonus word

bonus word

Building Spelling Skills

NAME

WEEK 10

feature
creature
pitcher
lecturer
bleachers
archery
picturesque
preacher
fixture
puncture
leisure
pleasure
closure
fracture
moisture
catcher
seizure
natural

bonus word

bonus word

cut

Building Spelling Skills

NAME

WEEK 11

enough
physical
symphony
coughing
briefly
pamphlet
chieftain
amphibian
efficient
flexible
turmoil
typhoid
ointment
voyager
boycott
loyalty
corduroy
oily

bonus word

bonus word

cut

Building Spelling Skills

NAME

WEEK 12

honorable
doorknob
chalkboard
plumber
condemn
gnarled
sighed
scented
trestle
drought
doubt
acknowledge
wholesome
castle
exhaustion
shipwreck
pneumonia
wrestling

bonus word

bonus word

Building Spelling Skills

NAME

WEEK 13

magazine
algebra
antenna
efficiency
opinion
appearance
colonel
absolutely
national
argument
article
orchestra
warning
architect
formula
participant
shortage
ordinary

______ bonus word

______ bonus word

cut

Building Spelling Skills

NAME

WEEK 14

they're
their
reign
rein
incite
insight
borough
burrow
censor
sensor
chorale
corral
all ready
already
assistance
assistants
broach
brooch

______ bonus word

______ bonus word

cut

Building Spelling Skills

NAME

WEEK 15

expression
collision
application
prediction
persuasion
succession
beautician
musician
starvation
reaction
violation
imitation
observation
separation
estimation
ambition
action
solution

______ bonus word

______ bonus word

Building Spelling Skills

NAME

WEEK 16

loose
lose
cease
seize
finely
finally
through
thorough
stationery
stationary
patients
patience
affect
effect
principal
principle
hostel
hostile

bonus word

bonus word

cut

Building Spelling Skills

NAME

WEEK 17

magnificent
obedient
persistent
equivalent
fluorescent
incident
valiant
brilliant
ignorant
significant
reluctant
attendant
dormant
vigilant
radiant
immigrant
accident
confident

bonus word

bonus word

cut

Building Spelling Skills

NAME

WEEK 18

permission
impatient
dictionary
delicious
ocean
physician
establish
ambitious
surely
magician
conversation
inertia
ashes
official
sufficient
glacier
brochure
friendship

bonus word

bonus word

Building Spelling Skills

NAME

WEEK 19

audible
plausible
indelible
compatible
credible
sensible
profitable
durable
lovable
acceptable
predictable
changeable
infectious
curious
cautious
precious
vicious
numerous

bonus word

bonus word

cut

Building Spelling Skills

NAME

WEEK 20

mosquitoes
varieties
beliefs
grievances
schedules
echoes
thieves
journeys
halves
passersby
substances
orchestras
pharmacies
sergeants
tomatoes
boundaries
instruments
encyclopedias

bonus word

bonus word

cut

Building Spelling Skills

NAME

WEEK 21

government
judgment
experiment
development
amazement
enjoyment
painless
tireless
humorless
effortless
powerless
colorless
successful
doubtful
cheerful
careful
grateful
thoughtful

bonus word

bonus word

Building Spelling Skills

NAME

WEEK 22

immature
immobile
imperfect
immortal
immediate
unsure
unlikely
unreliable
uncertain
inability
inanimate
incautious
independent
inconvenient
underneath
undercover
underage
underestimate

bonus word

bonus word

cut

Building Spelling Skills

NAME

WEEK 23

geology
geography
geologist
graphite
autograph
photograph
biopsy
biology
biography
biosphere
transact
enact
actor
react
import
transport
portable
export

bonus word

bonus word

cut

Building Spelling Skills

NAME

WEEK 24

admitted
answered
concluded
exclaimed
insisted
remarked
whispered
advised
blurted
commented
demanded
explained
mentioned
observed
replied
whined
screamed
inquired

bonus word

bonus word

Building Spelling Skills

NAME

WEEK 25

especially
immediately
permanently
temporarily
perfectly
sincerely
buoyancy
truancy
vacancy
citizenship
partnership
ownership
championship
membership
strengthen
lengthen
frighten
fasten

bonus word

bonus word

cut

Building Spelling Skills

NAME

WEEK 26

misspell
misbehave
misfortune
misdirect
dishonest
discourage
disagree
disgrace
antisocial
antifreeze
antiseptic
reappear
rewrite
recede
nonsense
nonconformist
nonexistent
nonfiction

bonus word

bonus word

cut

Building Spelling Skills

NAME

WEEK 27

punctual
ancient
miniature
stupendous
inquisitive
wasteful
zealous
obnoxious
pathetic
obsolete
ridiculous
genuine
congenial
optimistic
reliable
abundant
meager
sparse

bonus word

bonus word

Building Spelling Skills

NAME

WEEK 28

binocular
bicentennial
bilingual
bipedal
triceps
triathlon
triad
triplicate
unicorn
unify
union
unique
semicircle
semicolon
semiannual
centipede
century
centennial

bonus word

bonus word

cut

Building Spelling Skills

NAME

WEEK 29

eruption
interrupt
bankrupt
rupture
spectator
suspect
respect
spectacle
signature
insignia
signal
microscope
telescope
stethoscope
uniform
reformat
formal
transform

bonus word

bonus word

cut

Building Spelling Skills

NAME

WEEK 30

environment
Antarctica
international
peninsula
constitutional
bureaucracy
patriotism
hemisphere
archeology
atmospheric
cartographer
coordinates
parallelogram
perpendicular
rhombus
theorem
polyhedron
circumference

bonus word

bonus word

Building
WEEK 1
Spelling
Skills

Spelling List

This Week's Focus:
- Spell words with the short and long **a** vowel sounds

STEP 1 Read and Spell	STEP 2 Copy and Spell	STEP 3 Cover and Spell
1. plague		
2. straight		
3. freighter		
4. waist		
5. agent		
6. acre		
7. mayor		
8. obey		
9. restrain		
10. campaign		
11. persuade		
12. survey		
13. anticipate		
14. famous		
15. fragile		
16. axle		
17. aunt		
18. aptitude		
19. ______ bonus word		
20. ______ bonus word		

fold

Word Meaning

Complete the crossword puzzle using spelling words.

Across
1. to hold back
3. a ship that carries cargo
4. the elected head of a city or town
7. not crooked
8. to do what you are told
10. a person who represents another
11. to talk someone into doing something

Down
2. to look forward to
3. easily broken
5. a measure of land
6. a natural ability
7. to look over; to examine
9. the part of the body between the ribs and the hips
10. a rod connecting two wheels

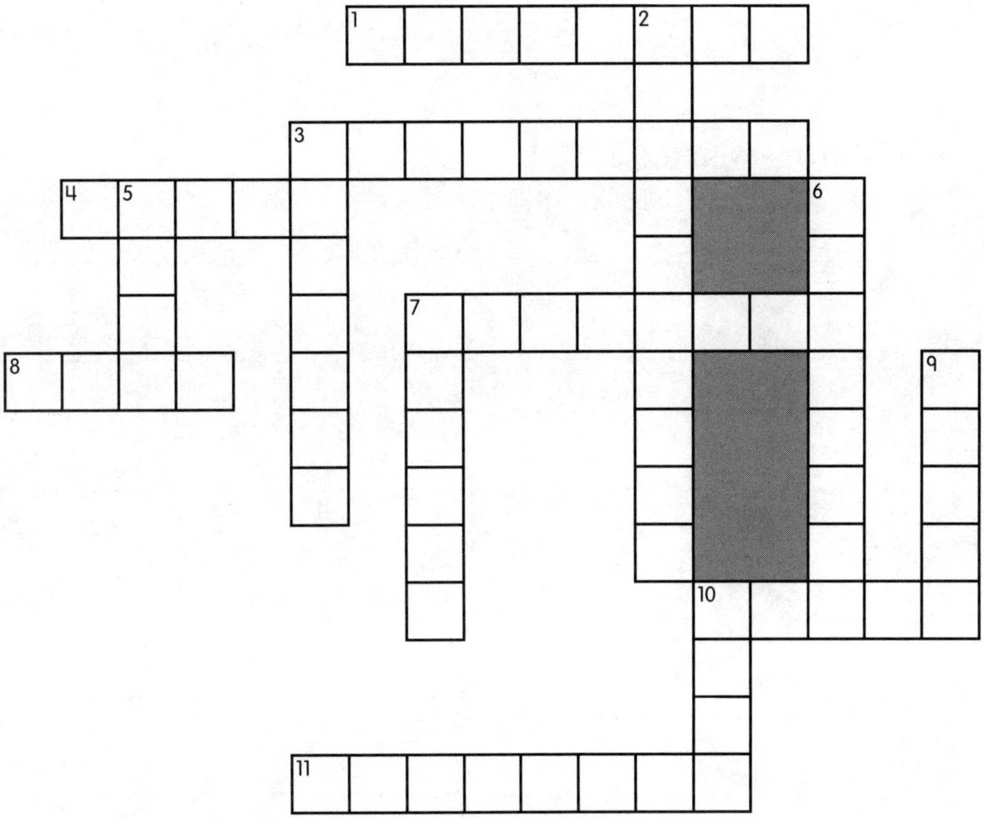

My Spelling Dictation

Write the sentences. Circle the spelling words.

1. ______________________________

____

2. ______________________________

____

Word Study

List spelling words that have the sound of long **a**.
Then circle the letters that make the long **a** sound.

waist	____________	____________
____________	____________	____________
____________	____________	____________
____________	____________	____________
____________	____________	

Write spelling words that rhyme with these words.

1. taste ____________
2. weight ____________
3. later ____________
4. afraid ____________

Match syllables to make spelling words.
Write the complete words on the lines.

1. fra	vey	1. fragile
2. fa	gent	2. ____________
3. sur	bey	3. ____________
4. cam	mous	4. ____________
5. re	cre	5. ____________
6. o	gile	6. ____________
7. a	paign	7. ____________
8. a	strain	8. ____________

Edit for Spelling

Circle the word in each row that is spelled correctly.

1. aunt	ent	aunnt
2. survay	servey	survey
3. axcle	axle	axcel
4. famiss	famouse	famous
5. persuade	pursuade	purrsuade
6. campane	campain	campaign
7. plage	plague	plaigue
8. aptitude	apptitude	aptatude
9. fraggile	frajile	fragile
10. akre	acre	acur
11. obay	obey	obbey
12. anticipate	antisipate	anticapate

Circle the misspelled words in the sentences. Write them correctly on the lines.

1. I tried to purswade my annt to let me work on her campane.

   ______________________ ______________________ ______________________

2. Even the faymous mair has to obay the law.

   ______________________ ______________________ ______________________

3. The agunt from the land office has come to servay the akcer.

   ______________________ ______________________ ______________________

4. The fragill old woman has strate hair that reaches to her waiste.

   ______________________ ______________________ ______________________

Building Spelling Skills WEEK 2

Spelling List

This Week's Focus:

- Spell words with the short and long **e** vowel sounds

STEP 1 Read and Spell | STEP 2 Copy and Spell | STEP 3 Cover and Spell

(fold)

1. hockey
2. received
3. neither
4. believe
5. achievement
6. equality
7. referee
8. pleasant
9. illegal
10. nominee
11. electricity
12. frequent
13. entry
14. eagerly
15. pique
16. easel
17. abbreviate
18. tedious
19. ________ bonus word
20. ________ bonus word

Word Meaning

Fill in the blanks with spelling words.

1. The ____________ stopped the ____________ game because of ____________ moves by the players.

2. ____________ of my parents could ____________ that I finished the task so quickly.

3. Elizabeth ____________ an award for her great ____________.

4. Clark ____________ approached his ____________ and began to paint.

5. Our state is suffering from ____________ shortages of ____________.

6. The ____________ for school council believes in ____________ for all students.

My Spelling Dictation

Write the sentences. Circle the spelling words.

1. ____

____

2. ____

____

Word Study

These vowel combinations can make the short or long **e** sound. Fill in the missing letter or letters to make spelling words.

ie ee e ea ei ey y

1. ill______gal
2. n______ther
3. refer______
4. ______sel
5. pl______sant
6. abbr______viate
7. rec______ved
8. fr______quent
9. bel______ve
10. ach______vement
11. t______dious
12. entr______
13. hock______
14. ______quality
15. nomin______
16. ______lectricit______
17. ______gerly

Write the spelling word that rhymes with **week**. ____________

Count the syllables in each word. Write the number on the line.

1. hockey __2__
2. abbreviate ______
3. tedious ______
4. referee ______
5. equality ______
6. frequent ______
7. believe ______
8. nominee ______
9. electricity ______

Edit for Spelling

Circle the word in each row that is spelled correctly.

1.	receeved	recieved	received
2.	tedious	teidious	teedious
3.	illeegal	illeigal	illegal
4.	beleeve	believe	beleive
5.	eagerly	eegerly	eagerley
6.	freequent	freaquant	frequent
7.	hockey	hocky	howcky
8.	electricitey	electricity	electriciti
9.	neither	niether	neather
10.	abbriviate	abreviate	abbreviate
11.	achevement	acheivement	achievement
12.	eesal	easel	eassel

Circle the misspelled words in the sentences. Write them correctly on the lines.

1. When I was at college, I recieved freaquant letters from my sister.

   ____________________ ____________________

2. The referree made his calls in a pleazant manner.

   ____________________ ____________________

3. So that our report would not be teedious, Jill and I used colorful charts which we displayed on an eesal.

   ____________________ ____________________

4. The nominey spoke eagerley to reporters about his plan to reduce the price of electricitee.

   ____________________ ____________________ ____________________

Building **Spelling** Skills WEEK 3

Spelling List

This Week's Focus:

- Spell words with the short and long **o** vowel sounds
- Recognize the /**aw**/ sound spelled **o**

STEP 1 Read and Spell	STEP 2 Copy and Spell	STEP 3 Cover and Spell
1. although		
2. moment		
3. goalie		
4. poem		
5. poetry		
6. approach		
7. ceremony		
8. stowaway		
9. trolley		
10. oxygen		
11. often		
12. officer		
13. obstacle		
14. envelope		
15. proverb		
16. antelope		
17. molecule		
18. obstinate		
19. ____ bonus word		
20. ____ bonus word		

fold

Word Meaning

Fill in the blanks with spelling words.

1. The ________________ scrambled over an ________________ as he chased the ________________ around the ship.

2. Sandra slipped the ________________ she was planning to read at the ________________ in an ________________.

3. ________________ the ________________ was exhausted, he did not relax for a ________________ during the game.

4. My grandfather ________________ likes to recite his favorite ________________.

5. We decided to take the ________________ up the hill instead of walk.

6. The ________________ ________________ did not want to go into the fenced area.

My Spelling Dictation

Write the sentences. Circle the spelling words.

1. ____

____

2. ____

____

Word Study

Write the spelling words in the correct boxes.

although	molecule	antelope	obstacle	trolley	poetry
moment	goalie	ceremony	proverb	approach	
obstinate	stowaway	oxygen	envelope	poem	

long **o** as in **hope**	short **o** as in **hot**

Count the syllables in each word. Write the number on the line.

1. oxygen ________
2. goalie ________
3. envelope ________
4. although ________
5. proverb ________
6. obstinate ________
7. ceremony ________
8. officer ________
9. molecule ________
10. stowaway ________
11. approach ________
12. poem ________

Edit for Spelling

Circle the word in each row that is spelled correctly.

1.	envalope	envelope	envellope
2.	oficer	officerr	officer
3.	poetry	poitry	potery
4.	althogh	althow	although
5.	ceremony	seremony	cerremony
6.	oxigen	oxygin	oxygen
7.	obstinate	obstinant	obbstinate
8.	approach	aproach	approch
9.	offen	often	oftin
10.	momint	moment	momment
11.	obstackle	obbstacle	obstacle
12.	mollecule	molicule	molecule

Circle the misspelled words in the sentences. Write them correctly on the lines.

1. The offiser took oxigen to the injured goaly.

   ____________ ____________ ____________

2. The cerramony was over in only a momant.

   ____________ ____________

3. Althogh the man was a stoaway, he wrote a beautiful poim.

   ____________ ____________ ____________

4. Simon could not approch the antilope because it ran too fast.

   ____________ ____________

Building
WEEK 4
Spelling
Skills

Spelling List

This Week's Focus:
- Spell words with the short and long **i** vowel sounds

STEP 1 Read and Spell	STEP 2 Copy and Spell	STEP 3 Cover and Spell
1. buyer		
2. instant		
3. quietly		
4. plight		
5. describe		
6. acquire		
7. typhoon		
8. twice		
9. lithe		
10. scientific		
11. blind		
12. decipher		
13. distinct		
14. xylophone		
15. glimpse		
16. pliable		
17. slight		
18. friction		
19. ______ bonus word		
20. ______ bonus word		

fold

Word Meaning

Complete the crossword puzzle using spelling words.

Down

1. in a noiseless way
2. the rubbing of one thing against another
4. different or set apart
6. a hurricane
7. to tell about
10. a brief look
13. small

Across

3. a sad or bad situation
5. immediate
8. relating to science
9. two times
11. unable to see
12. to figure out or make sense of
14. easily bent
15. flexible and graceful

My Spelling Dictation

Write the sentences. Circle the spelling words.

1. ______________________________

____

2. ______________________________

____

Word Study

Circle the letter or letters that make the long **i** sound.

plight	twice	decipher
slight	describe	typhoon
lithe	blind	xylophone
buyer	pliable	quietly

Divide these words into syllables.
Write the syllables on the lines.

1. instant ____in stant____
2. buyer ____________
3. distinct ____________
4. friction ____________
5. acquire ____________
6. describe ____________
7. typhoon ____________
8. pliable ____________
9. quietly ____________
10. scientific ____________
11. xylophone ____________

Edit for Spelling

Circle the word in each row that is spelled correctly.

1.	instint	instant	instent
2.	plyable	pliyable	pliable
3.	buyer	byer	buyo
4.	twice	twict	twis
5.	ackwire	acquire	aquir
6.	discribe	desscribe	describe
7.	zylofone	xylophone	xilophone
8.	decipher	decifer	deciphar
9.	frictsion	fricsion	friction
10.	quitely	quitly	quietly
11.	distinct	disstinct	distenct
12.	sciantific	sientific	scientific

Circle the misspelled words in the sentences. Write them correctly on the lines.

1. Yellow buttercups swayed quitely in the sliet breeze.

   ______________________ ______________________

2. I made instint oatmeal for breakfast twise this week.

   ______________________ ______________________

3. The buyor wanted to aquire some scientiffic equipment.

   ______________________ ______________________ ______________________

4. It is hard to discribe the plite of the island people after the typhune.

   ______________________ ______________________ ______________________

Building Spelling Skills WEEK 5

Spelling List

This Week's Focus:

- Spell words with the short and long **u** vowel sounds

STEP 1 Read and Spell | STEP 2 Copy and Spell | STEP 3 Cover and Spell

fold

1. country
2. does
3. once
4. beautiful
5. unusual
6. unit
7. fugitive
8. menu
9. utilize
10. sculpture
11. valuable
12. thumbprint
13. museum
14. universe
15. luxury
16. sulfur
17. customary
18. suffocate
19. ____________ bonus word
20. ____________ bonus word

Word Meaning

Match each word to its meaning. Write the letter on the line.

_____	1. valuable	a. to use
_____	2. fugitive	b. a yellow chemical element
_____	3. suffocate	c. out of the ordinary
_____	4. luxury	d. someone who has run away or escaped
_____	5. sculpture	e. usual; normal
_____	6. unusual	f. to deprive of air
_____	7. customary	g. worth a great deal of money
_____	8. utilize	h. one of the parts of a whole
_____	9. sulfur	i. a statue or figure formed by molding or cutting
_____	10. beautiful	j. a list of food available at a restaurant
_____	11. menu	k. everything that exists
_____	12. museum	l. something that is nice to have, but not necessary
_____	13. unit	m. very lovely
_____	14. universe	n. a building where objects of interest and value are kept and displayed

My Spelling Dictation

Write the sentences. Circle the spelling words.

1. ____

____

2. ____

____

Word Study

Draw a line under the words that have the long **u** sound.

museum	universe	customary
does	menu	luxury
thumbprint	sulfur	unit
unusual	utilize	valuable
country	beautiful	fugitive

Write the plural form of each word.
Check the box that shows how you changed the word.

		add **s**	change **y** to **i** and add **es**
1. country	countries		✔
2. unit			
3. fugitive			
4. sculpture			
5. thumbprint			
6. museum			
7. luxury			

Edit for Spelling

Circle the word in each row that is spelled correctly.

1.	lucksury	luxurie	luxury
2.	suffocate	sufocate	suffocat
3.	menyu	menu	minu
4.	utelice	yutilize	utilize

Circle the 12 misspelled words below.
Write the words correctly on the lines.

Mystery at the Museum

News flash! A clever criminal broke into the museam last night and stole a valluable sculptoor. The beuatiful statue wonce stood in front of a palace in the countrie of France. The police detective dous not know how the thief was able to get away with his crime, as all of the customery security measures were in place. The guards reported no unnusual activity during the night. The only clue is a large thumprint on the glass case that held the statue. The police chief says that he will go to the ends of the univurse to find the fujitive.

Building **Spelling** Skills WEEK 6

Spelling List

This Week's Focus:
- Spell words with double letters
- Spell words with the **/aw/** sound

STEP 1 Read and Spell | STEP 2 Copy and Spell | STEP 3 Cover and Spell

fold

1. occurrence
2. embarrass
3. occasion
4. symmetry
5. recommend
6. exaggerate
7. terrain
8. barricade
9. alliance
10. applaud
11. hooray
12. opportunity
13. opposite
14. daughter
15. authentic
16. awkward
17. brought
18. because
19. ________ bonus word
20. ________ bonus word

Word Meaning

Fill in the blanks with spelling words.

1. Rosalie began to ____________ wildly when her ____________ appeared on the stage.

2. The astronaut had a unique ____________ to study the ____________ on the planet Mars.

3. I would ____________ that you learn not to ____________ when you tell stories ____________ people will not believe you.

4. James ____________ some hay to the ____________ colt.

5. The police set up a ____________ for the parade route.

6. Gavin shouted, "____________!" when he found out the old coin was ____________.

7. If it snows, we will observe the ____________ in snowflakes.

My Spelling Dictation

Write the sentences. Circle the spelling words.

1. ______________________________

____

2. ______________________________

____

Word Study

Fill in the missing letters.

au aw ou

1. appl______d
2. d______ghter
3. br______ght
4. ______kward
5. bec______se
6. ______thentic

Fill in the missing letters.

pp mm rr ss cc gg ll

1. o______osite
2. o______u______ence
3. emba______a______
4. o______ortunity
5. o______asion
6. reco______end
7. sy______etry
8. exa______erate
9. ba______icade
10. te______ain
11. a______iance

Count the syllables in each word. Write the number on the line.

1. brought ______
2. opportunity ______
3. awkward ______
4. recommend ______
5. authentic ______
6. exaggerate ______

Edit for Spelling

Circle each word that is spelled correctly.

symmetry	doughter	aukward	oposite
embarass	occassion	barricade	occurence
awthentic	alliance	oportunity	exagerate
reccomend	brout	because	applaud

Circle the misspelled words in the sentences. Write them correctly on the lines.

1. The owkward boy kept tripping as he hiked across the rugged terrane.

   ____________________ ____________________

2. Our family had an oppertunity to see the awthentic belongings of Abraham Lincoln.

   ____________________ ____________________

3. Senator Rogers formed an aliance with Senator Davidson, even though they hold oposite positions on many issues.

   ____________________ ____________________

4. The audience began to stamp their feet, aplaud enthusiastically, and shout “horay” at the top of their lungs.

   ____________________ ____________________

5. On the ocassion of your birthday, we will try not to embarass you.

   ____________________ ____________________

Building WEEK 7 **Spelling** Skills

Spelling List

This Week's Focus:

- Spell words with the endings **-ed**, **-ing**, **-er**, and **-est**
- Practice adding endings to base words

STEP 1 Read and Spell	STEP 2 Copy and Spell	STEP 3 Cover and Spell
1. gestured	________	________
2. gesturing	________	________
3. hesitated	________	________
4. hesitating	________	________
5. studied	________	________
6. studying	________	________
7. prescribed	________	________
8. prescribing	________	________
9. skied	________	________
10. skiing	________	________
11. lonelier	________	________
12. loneliest	________	________
13. friendlier	________	________
14. friendliest	________	________
15. cleaner	________	________
16. cleanest	________	________
17. angrier	________	________
18. angriest	________	________
19. ________ bonus word	________	________
20. ________ bonus word	________	________

fold

Word Meaning

Answer the questions using spelling words.

1. Which spelling word is an antonym for **dirtiest**? ______________

2. Which spelling word means...?

   a. used a movement of the head or body to convey meaning ______________

   b. tried to learn ______________

   c. paused because of fear or indecision ______________

3. Which spelling word rhymes with...?

   a. freed ______________ b. meaner ______________

4. Which spelling words are superlatives?

   ______________ ______________

   ______________ ______________

5. Which spelling word names an activity that is fun to do on snow or water? ______________

My Spelling Dictation

Write the sentences. Circle the spelling words.

1. ____

   ____

2. ____

   ____

Word Study

Add **ing** to the base words.
Check the box that shows how you changed the word.

		no change	drop **e**
1. gesture	______		
2. hesitate	______		
3. study	______		
4. prescribe	______		
5. ski	______		

Add **er** to the base words.
Check the box that shows how you changed the word.

		no change	change **y** to **i**
1. clean	______		
2. lonely	______		
3. friendly	______		
4. angry	______		

Add an ending to each word so that the sentence makes sense.

1. Hannah is the ______ girl in the class.
(friendly)

2. The speaker is ______ with his hands to emphasize his point.
(gesture)

3. Dad was ______ than I have ever seen him before.
(angry)

4. Doctor Forbes ______ some medication for the sick child.
(prescribe)

Edit for Spelling

Write each word correctly.

1. gesturred ______
2. angryer ______
3. lonelyest ______
4. prescribbing ______
5. hesitatied ______
6. cleanner ______
7. friendlyier ______
8. studyed ______
9. sking ______
10. cleaniest ______

Circle the misspelled words in the sentences. Write them correctly on the lines.

1. Michelle was studdying all by herself, and she felt like the lonnliest person in the world.

   ______ ______

2. Ronald hesittated before he skiied down the difficult slope.

   ______ ______

3. The manager wants to hire the friendlyist and cleannest people he can find to work in the restaurant.

   ______ ______

4. Marcus was the angryest one at the meeting, and he was gestureing wildly as he spoke, flinging his arms around without hesitateing to see if anyone was in his way.

   ______ ______ ______

Building Spelling Skills WEEK 8

Spelling List

This Week's Focus:

- Spell compound words

Step 1 Read and Spell	Step 2 Copy and Spell	Step 3 Cover and Spell
1. everybody		
2. anywhere		
3. knowledge		
4. brainstorm		
5. stomachache		
6. outstanding		
7. sweatshirt		
8. videotape		
9. meanwhile		
10. old-fashioned		
11. long-distance		
12. duffel bag		
13. child's play		
14. absent-minded		
15. daybreak		
16. high school		
17. headquarters		
18. themselves		
19. ______ bonus word		
20. ______ bonus word		

fold

Word Meaning

Notice that a compound word does not have to be written as one word. Sometimes the parts of a compound word are joined by a hyphen; sometimes they are two separate words.

Match each spelling word to its meaning. Write the letter on the line.

_____ 1. everybody	a. a sick feeling in your belly
_____ 2. anywhere	b. something that is simple and easy to do
_____ 3. brainstorm	c. dawn
_____ 4. outstanding	d. related to old ways of doing things; outdated
_____ 5. sweatshirt	e. a large canvas bag
_____ 6. meanwhile	f. the main office
_____ 7. old-fashioned	g. all people
_____ 8. duffel bag	h. any place or point
_____ 9. child's play	i. forgetful
_____ 10. absent-minded	j. a heavy cotton pullover
_____ 11. daybreak	k. unusual; excellent
_____ 12. headquarters	l. a sudden, creative idea
_____ 13. stomachache	m. at the same time

My Spelling Dictation

Write the sentences. Circle the spelling words.

1. ____

____

2. ____

____

Word Study

Use one word from each box to make compound words.
Cross out each word as you use it.
Check the spelling list to make sure that you form the compound words correctly.

~~every~~	ache
any	selves
brain	quarters
day	school
high	while
head	break
them	~~body~~
mean	ledge
stomach	where
know	storm

1. everybody
2. ______
3. ______
4. ______
5. ______
6. ______
7. ______
8. ______
9. ______
10. ______

Circle the letter or letters that make the long vowel sounds in the words below. Then circle the sound that the letter or letters make. Some words will have more than one sound circled.

1. videotape	a	e	i	o	u
2. meanwhile	a	e	i	o	u
3. daybreak	a	e	i	o	u
4. high school	a	e	i	o	u
5. absent-minded	a	e	i	o	u
6. old-fashioned	a	e	i	o	u
7. stomachache	a	e	i	o	u
8. brainstorm	a	e	i	o	u

Edit for Spelling

Circle the word in each row that is spelled correctly.

1. every body	every-body	everybody
2. duffel bag	duffel-bag	duffelbag
3. brain storm	brain-storm	brainstorm
4. out standing	out-standing	outstanding
5. long distance	long-distance	longdistance
6. sweat shirt	sweat-shirt	sweatshirt
7. videotape	video-tape	video tape
8. head quarters	head-quarters	headquarters
9. absent minded	absent-minded	absentminded
10. old fashioned	old-fashioned	oldfashioned

Circle the misspelled words in the sentences. Write them correctly on the lines.

1. I woke up at day-break with a stomach ache.

   ____________________ ____________________

2. Shauna didn't want to go any where while she was wearing her ragged old sweat-shirt.

   ____________________ ____________________

3. Uncle Herb told every body to make them-selves at home.

   ____________________ ____________________

4. When Joe got back to head-quarters, he made several longdistance calls to discuss his latest brain storm.

   ____________________ ____________________ ____________________

Building **Spelling** Skills WEEK 9

Spelling List

This Week's Focus:
- Spell words with the /**ur**/ sound

STEP 1 Read and Spell	STEP 2 Copy and Spell	STEP 3 Cover and Spell
1. favorite		
2. traitor		
3. circuit		
4. circumvent		
5. rehearse		
6. courtesy		
7. courteous		
8. humor		
9. humorous		
10. energy		
11. energetic		
12. courage		
13. courageous		
14. similar		
15. grammar		
16. worthy		
17. earthworm		
18. earnestly		
19. ______ bonus word		
20. ______ bonus word		

fold

Word Meaning

Complete the crossword puzzle using spelling words.

Down

1. someone who betrays you
2. to practice
3. to go around
4. sincerely
5. the one you like best
7. bravery
9. a system of wires that electricity flows through

Across

4. full of energy
6. politeness
8. a worm that lives in the soil
10. alike
11. funny
12. having value; important

My Spelling Dictation

Write the sentences. Circle the spelling words.

1. ______________________________

____

2. ______________________________

____

Word Study

Circle the letters that make the /**ur**/ sound.

favorite	traitor	earthworm
worthy	grammar	courage
courtesy	rehearse	circuit
energy	earnestly	similar

How many ways was /**ur**/ spelled? ________

Match syllables to make spelling words.
Write the complete words on the lines.

1. trai	cuit		1. traitor
2. cir	worm		2. ________
3. hu	age		3. ________
4. wor	tor		4. ________
5. earth	mor		5. ________
6. cour	thy		6. ________
7. cou	vor	ly	7. ________
8. earn	er	ite	8. ________
9. cir	cum	gy	9. ________
10. fa	ra	vent	10. ________
11. en	est	geous	11. ________

Edit for Spelling

Circle the 12 misspelled words in this paragraph.
Write them correctly on the lines below.

My Uncle Hank

Last summer, my parents sent me off for a two-week visit with Uncle Hank. Uncle Hank is my faverite uncle. He runs an earthwirm farm. Hank has had a lot of birthdays and has plenty of wrinkles, but if you call him old, he'll call you a traytor and laugh. He is still full of life and enerjy. His grammer isn't perfect, but he knows lots of humerous stories and tall tales. He will look you in the eye and tell you very urnestly about the time he wrestled a 12-foot-long alligator, fought off a whole family of grizzly bears, or a semilar curagous, hair-raising adventure! There is no lack of fun around Uncle Hank! Before he retired, Uncle Hank was a circcuit judge. My dad says he is a wourthy man and a curteous gentleman. I wish everyone could have an Uncle Hank!

________________	________________
________________	________________
________________	________________
________________	________________
________________	________________
________________	________________

Building Spelling Skills WEEK 10

Spelling List

This Week's Focus:

- Spell words with the **/cher/** and **/zher/** sounds

STEP 1 Read and Spell	STEP 2 Copy and Spell	STEP 3 Cover and Spell
1. feature		
2. creature		
3. pitcher		
4. lecturer		
5. bleachers		
6. archery		
7. picturesque		
8. preacher		
9. fixture		
10. puncture		
11. leisure		
12. pleasure		
13. closure		
14. fracture		
15. moisture		
16. catcher		
17. seizure		
18. natural		
19. ______ bonus word		
20. ______ bonus word		

fold

Word Meaning

Fill in the blanks with spelling words.

1. It is a great ____________ to sit on ____________ and watch a fine ____________ fling the ball across home plate.

2. The ____________ lessons were held in a lovely, ____________ park.

3. Due to a ____________ in his tire, Jacob fell off his bike and suffered a ____________ in his right arm.

4. The biology ____________ explained that each ____________ has an important place in the ____________ world.

5. Grandpa wants it to rain because his garden needs the ____________.

6. The museum will ____________ the famous painting as a permanent ____________ in its collection.

My Spelling Dictation

Write the sentences. Circle the spelling words.

1. ____

____

2. ____

____

Word Study

Fill in the missing letters to make spelling words.

cher tur sur zur

1. fea__________e	5. frac__________e	9. pit__________
2. sei__________e	6. na__________al	10. lei__________e
3. cat__________	7. ar__________y	11. clo__________e
4. punc__________e	8. fix__________e	12. lec__________er

Divide these words into syllables. Write the syllables on the lines.

1. preacher ____________________
2. moisture ____________________
3. seizure ____________________
4. bleachers ____________________
5. pleasure ____________________
6. fracture ____________________
7. archery ____________________
8. picturesque ____________________
9. lecturer ____________________
10. natural ____________________

Edit for Spelling

Circle the words that are spelled correctly.

puncsure	moischer	natural	feature
preasher	catcher	fracsure	pleazure
creature	archury	closure	fixture

Circle the misspelled words in the sentences.
Write them correctly on the lines.

1. The preecher likes to practice artchery in his leizure time.

   __________ __________ __________

2. We were all saddened by the clozure of the pitcheresk park.

   __________ __________

3. Beads of moistur formed on the outside of the cold pitchure.

   __________ __________

4. There was a large, slimy creecher in the scary featcher movie.

   __________ __________

5. The lecsurer was so dull that we did not get any plezsure from his talk.

   __________ __________

Building Spelling Skills WEEK 11

Spelling List

This Week's Focus:

- Spell words with the /f/ sound spelled **f**, **gh**, **ph**, and **ff**
- Spell words with the /**oi**/ sound spelled **oi** and **oy**

STEP 1 Read and Spell	STEP 2 Copy and Spell	STEP 3 Cover and Spell
1. enough		
2. physical		
3. symphony		
4. coughing		
5. briefly		
6. pamphlet		
7. chieftain		
8. amphibian		
9. efficient		
10. flexible		
11. turmoil		
12. typhoid		
13. ointment		
14. voyager		
15. boycott		
16. loyalty		
17. corduroy		
18. oily		
19. ______ bonus word		
20. ______ bonus word		

fold

Word Meaning

Answer these questions using spelling words.

1. Which spelling word names a disease? ____________
2. Which spelling word names a type of fabric? ____________
3. Which spelling word names a kind of animal? ____________
4. Which spelling word means the opposite of...?
   a. at length ____________
   b. rigid ____________
   c. tranquility ____________
5. Which spelling word names something you put on your skin? ____________
6. Which spelling word is a synonym for **brochure**? ____________
7. Which spelling word names a musical piece? ____________
8. Which spelling word means "to refuse to buy or use something"? ____________
9. Which spelling word names a quality you would like in a friend? ____________

My Spelling Dictation

Write the sentences. Circle the spelling words.

1. ____

____

2. ____

____

Word Study

Fill in the missing letter or letters to make spelling words.

oi oy

1. l______alty
2. ______ly
3. cordur______
4. typh______d
5. b______cott
6. v______ager
7. ______ntment
8. turm______l

f gh ph

1. ______ysical
2. chie______tain
3. ______lexible
4. sym______ony
5. am______ibian
6. enou______
7. pam______let
8. cou______ing

Write the spelling words that are synonyms for these words.

1. sufficient ____________
2. faithfulness ____________
3. medicinal cream ____________
4. greasy ____________
5. traveler ____________
6. commotion ____________
7. pliable ____________
8. working well ____________
9. leader ____________
10. in short ____________

Edit for Spelling

Circle the word in each row that is spelled correctly.

1.	oyly	oily	oilly
2.	voiager	voyiger	voyager
3.	enough	enouph	enouff
4.	simphony	symphony	symphonie
5.	physical	phisical	physicle
6.	ointment	oyntment	ointtment
7.	couphing	couffing	coughing
8.	cheiftain	chieftain	chieftan
9.	amfibian	amphibbian	amphibian
10.	efficient	eficient	efficeint
11.	flexable	flexible	phlexible
12.	loialty	loyalty	loyelty

Circle the misspelled words in the sentences. Write them correctly on the lines.

1. This amfibian has strong, flexable back legs.

_____________________ _____________________

2. The conductor began coffing during the simphony.

_____________________ _____________________

3. I got my corduroie pants very oyly when I was fixing my car.

_____________________ _____________________

4. The voyiger must have enouph physicle strength for the long journey.

_____________________ _____________________ _____________________

Building Spelling Skills WEEK 12

Spelling List

This Week's Focus:

- Spell words with silent letters

STEP 1 Read and Spell | STEP 2 Copy and Spell | STEP 3 Cover and Spell

fold

1. honorable ______ ______
2. doorknob ______ ______
3. chalkboard ______ ______
4. plumber ______ ______
5. condemn ______ ______
6. gnarled ______ ______
7. sighed ______ ______
8. scented ______ ______
9. trestle ______ ______
10. drought ______ ______
11. doubt ______ ______
12. acknowledge ______ ______
13. wholesome ______ ______
14. castle ______ ______
15. exhaustion ______ ______
16. shipwreck ______ ______
17. pneumonia ______ ______
18. wrestling ______ ______
19. ______ (bonus word) ______ ______
20. ______ (bonus word) ______ ______

Word Meaning

Answer these questions using spelling words.

1. Which spelling words are opposites of these words?

   a. odorless ______________ c. certainty ______________

   b. acquit ______________ d. deny ______________

2. Which spelling words are compound words?

   ______________ ______________ ______________

3. Which spelling words mean about the same as these words?

   a. virtuous ______________ c. crooked ______________

   b. tiredness ______________ d. healthy ______________

4. Which spelling word means...?

   a. a disease of the lungs ______________

   b. exhaled heavily ______________

   c. struggling or fighting ______________

   d. a long dry spell ______________

   e. a large medieval stronghold ______________

   f. a framework built to carry railroad tracks ______________

My Spelling Dictation

Write the sentences. Circle the spelling words.

1. ____

   ____

2. ____

   ____

Word Study

Which of the underlined letters are silent? Circle them.

1. plumber
2. sighed
3. scented
4. shipwreck
5. condemn
6. castle
7. gnarled
8. pneumonia
9. doubt
10. doorknob
11. wholesome
12. honorable

Fill in the missing letter or letters to make spelling words.

1. cha________board
2. tre________le
3. drou________t
4. cond________
5. ac________owledge
6. ex________austion
7. ________estling
8. door________b

Below each group of words, write a word from the spelling list that has the same silent letter.

1	2	3	4
comb	knot	walked	hour
bomber	knight	talking	dishonest
thumb	unknown	caulk	herb
________	________	________	________

Edit for Spelling

Circle the 13 misspelled words below.
Write the words correctly on the lines.

The Honorable Captain

The ship's captain tried desperately to keep his boat afloat among the towering waves. He was nearing the point of utter exaustion. He side heavily and said to himself, "Without a dout, this is the worst storm I have ever seen." He watched his narled hands restling with the wheel, trying with all his might to avoid a shipreck. He did not want to condemm his sailors or his ship to such a terrible fate.

He struggled on through the night. In the morning, the winds ceased. The sun peeked out from behind the clouds. The air was fresh and sweetly sented. The captain could finally rest. He ate a holesome breakfast and then went right to bed. He was afraid he might have caught newmonia after being out in the moist, cold air all night.

When the ship returned safely to port, the king invited the captain to his cassle. He wanted to aknowledge the heroic efforts of the honerable old captain.

Building Spelling Skills WEEK 13

Spelling List

This Week's Focus:
- Spell words with the schwa sound,
- Review words with **r**-controlled vowel sounds

STEP 1 Read and Spell	STEP 2 Copy and Spell	STEP 3 Cover and Spell
1. magazine		
2. algebra		
3. antenna		
4. efficiency		
5. opinion		
6. appearance		
7. colonel		
8. absolutely		
9. national		
10. argument		
11. article		
12. orchestra		
13. warning		
14. architect		
15. formula		
16. participant		
17. shortage		
18. ordinary		
19. ______ bonus word		
20. ______ bonus word		

(fold)

Word Meaning

Complete the crossword puzzle using spelling words.

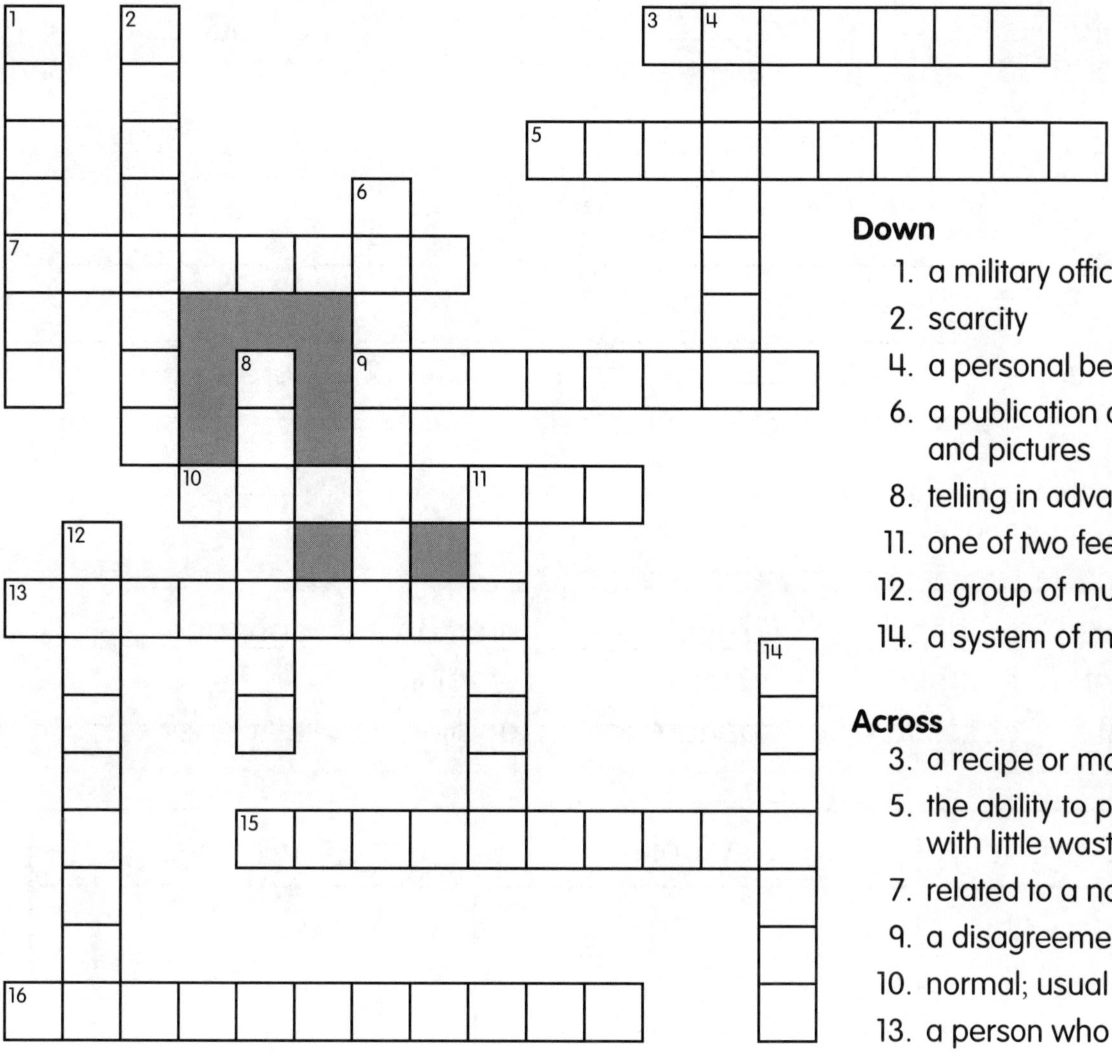

Down

1. a military officer
2. scarcity
4. a personal belief
6. a publication containing articles and pictures
8. telling in advance of danger
11. one of two feelers on an insect
12. a group of musicians
14. a system of mathematics

Across

3. a recipe or mathematical principle
5. the ability to produce something with little waste
7. related to a nation
9. a disagreement
10. normal; usual
13. a person who designs buildings
15. the way something looks
16. one who takes part

My Spelling Dictation

Write the sentences. Circle the spelling words.

1. ____

____

2. ____

____

Word Study

Fill in the missing syllables to make spelling words.

1. al_______bra
2. partici_______
3. _______chestra
4. ar_______ment
5. archi_______
6. abso_______ly
7. o_______ion
8. _______azine
9. nation_______
10. for_______la
11. _______pearance
12. short_______

Count the number of syllables in the words below.
Write the words in the correct boxes.

national	magazine	colonel	ordinary	shortage
participant	formula	architect	warning	article
argument	absolutely	appearance	opinion	efficiency

2 syllables	3 syllables	4 syllables

Edit for Spelling

Circle the misspelled words in the sentences.
Write them correctly on the lines.

1. My neighbor wrote an artacle for a nasional maggazine.

   ________________ ________________ ________________

2. In my opinyon, the orchistra performed quite well this evening.

   ________________ ________________

3. Janet learned a new formulla in her allgebra class today.

   ________________ ________________

4. The cornel absolutly refused to make an apearance on the television program.

   ________________ ________________ ________________

5. The arckitect was dismayed to learn that there was a shorttage of carpenters in the city.

   ________________ ________________

6. We examined the one bent antena on the ordenary butterfly.

   ________________ ________________

7. I gave my brother a worning that his behavior might lead to an arguement.

   ________________ ________________

Building Spelling Skills WEEK 14

Spelling List

This Week's Focus:
- Spell homophones

Step 1 Read and Spell	Step 2 Copy and Spell	Step 3 Cover and Spell
1. they're		
2. their		
3. reign		
4. rein		
5. incite		
6. insight		
7. borough		
8. burrow		
9. censor		
10. sensor		
11. chorale		
12. corral		
13. all ready		
14. already		
15. assistance		
16. assistants		
17. broach		
18. brooch		
19. ______ bonus word		
20. ______ bonus word		

fold

Word Meaning

Fill in the blanks with spelling words.

1. ____________ sure they will win the science fair, but I am not convinced that ____________ project is good enough.

2. The queen's ____________ pinned the emerald ____________ to the collar of her dress.

3. The biologist used a ____________ to track the animals back to their ____________.

4. Margie's grandmother lives in the ____________ of Brooklyn.

5. I will need your ____________ to get all the horses back into the ____________.

6. The first act of the cruel emperor's ____________ was to ____________ all the newspapers.

7. Laura was reluctant to ____________ the sensitive subject because she was afraid it might ____________ an argument.

My Spelling Dictation

Write the sentences. Circle the spelling words.

1. ____

____

2. ____

____

Word Study

Write the words in the correct boxes.

brooch	burrow	insight	reign
incite	broach	rein	borough

long **a**	long **o**	long **i**

Divide these words into syllables.
Write the syllables on the lines.

1. insight ________________
2. censor ________________
3. chorale ________________
4. burrow ________________
5. sensor ________________
6. incite ________________
7. corral ________________
8. borough ________________
9. assistance ________________
10. already ________________
11. assistants ________________

Edit for Spelling

Circle the words that are spelled correctly.

broach	raign	burow
corrale	chorale	assistents
insite	senssor	censor
borough	allready	thair
assistance	they're	rien

Circle the misspelled words in the sentences.
Write them correctly on the lines.

1. There trying to insite the crowd to violence.

   ____________________ ____________________

2. The people who want to go on the trail ride are alreddy down at the coral.

   ____________________ ____________________

3. My boss thanked me for my asistance and my inseight.

   ____________________ ____________________

4. The security agents jumped to they're feet when Grandmother's large broache set off the alarm on the airport's senser.

   ____________________ ____________________ ____________________

Building **Spelling** Skills WEEK 15

Spelling List

This Week's Focus:

- Spell words with the endings -**sion**, -**tion**, and -**cian**

STEP 1 Read and Spell	STEP 2 Copy and Spell	STEP 3 Cover and Spell
1. expression		
2. collision		
3. application		
4. prediction		
5. persuasion		
6. succession		
7. beautician		
8. musician		
9. starvation		
10. reaction		
11. violation		
12. imitation		
13. observation		
14. separation		
15. estimation		
16. ambition		
17. action		
18. solution		
19. ______ bonus word		
20. ______ bonus word		

(fold)

Word Meaning

Match each word to its meaning. Write the letter on the line.

_____	1. imitation	a. the action of seeing or noticing
_____	2. action	b. a person who plays a musical instrument
_____	3. collision	c. a copy or fake
_____	4. beautician	d. the act of suffering from a lack of food
_____	5. separation	e. a statement that something will happen
_____	6. solution	f. something that is done
_____	7. estimation	g. the act of showing or representing feeling
_____	8. violation	h. the act of making a guess
_____	9. ambition	i. a great desire to reach a goal
_____	10. musician	j. a crashing together
_____	11. starvation	k. a person who helps others with their appearance
_____	12. application	l. an answer
_____	13. prediction	m. a formal request for a job or position
_____	14. observation	n. the breaking of a rule or law
_____	15. expression	o. the act of parting company or dividing into groups

My Spelling Dictation

Write the sentences. Circle the spelling words.

1. ____

____

2. ____

____

Word Study

Add the ending **-tion** or **-sion** to change these verbs into nouns.
Some spelling changes will be necessary.

1. express ______________
2. imitate ______________
3. predict ______________
4. violate ______________
5. estimate ______________
6. separate ______________

Divide these words into syllables.
Write the syllables on the lines.

1. action ______________
2. ambition ______________
3. musician ______________
4. beautician ______________
5. succession ______________
6. starvation ______________
7. separation ______________
8. violation ______________
9. application ______________
10. observation ______________

Edit for Spelling

Circle the words that are spelled correctly.

ambition	beutician	collition
solution	accsion	violation
aplication	predicsion	estimation
observasion	reaction	musicion

Circle the misspelled words in the sentences.
Write them correctly on the lines.

1. After much persuation, the musitian offered to play for us.

   ________________ ________________

2. The prisoner's reactsion to food was a result of his long period of starvacion.

   ________________ ________________

3. I filled out a job aplication while the beautisian put a sollution on my hair.

   ________________ ________________ ________________

4. The woman who had been in the collisian had a frightened expresstion.

   ________________ ________________

5. With such ambitian, it is my estamacion that you will go far.

   ________________ ________________

Building Spelling Skills WEEK 16

Spelling List

This Week's Focus:
- Spell words with easily confused spellings
- Distinguish between homophones

STEP 1 Read and Spell	STEP 2 Copy and Spell	STEP 3 Cover and Spell
1. loose		
2. lose		
3. cease		
4. seize		
5. finely		
6. finally		
7. through		
8. thorough		
9. stationery		
10. stationary		
11. patients		
12. patience		
13. affect		
14. effect		
15. principal		
16. principle		
17. hostel		
18. hostile		
19. ______ bonus word		
20. ______ bonus word		

fold

Word Meaning

Answer these questions using spelling words.

1. Which spelling words name people?

_______________ _______________

2. Which spelling words contain the **/st/** sound?

_______________ _______________

_______________ _______________

3. Which spelling word is an antonym for...?

a. release _______________ c. find _______________

b. coarsely _______________ d. incomplete _______________

4. Which spelling word means...?

a. paper used for writing letters _______________

b. an inexpensive place for travelers to stay _______________

c. a basic rule or truth _______________

d. to stop _______________

e. to influence _______________

My Spelling Dictation

Write the sentences. Circle the spelling words.

1. ____

____

2. ____

____

Word Study

Fill in the blanks with spelling words.

1. Randall will probably ________________ his ________________ tooth very soon.

2. After chopping for an hour, I ________________ managed to dice the onions very ________________.

3. The desk clerk at the ________________ behaved in a ________________ manner to the students who were checking in.

4. Dr. Elliott has no ________________ with ________________ who refuse to follow his directions.

5. If you do not ________________ playing that music so loudly, I will have to ________________ your radio.

6. Our ________________, Mrs. Hatfield, is a woman of great ________________.

7. Janet looked ________________ every reference book in the library because she wanted to do a ________________ job on her report.

8. The rain will have a good ________________ on the plants but will not ________________ our plans to go to the movie.

Edit for Spelling

Circle the 13 misspelled words below.
Write the words correctly on the lines.

Dear Diary,

Our principle, Mr. Duncan, announced some exciting news yesterday! The senior class is going on a trip threw Italy. We have to do a lot of things to get ready. First, we have to write letters on school stationary explaining to our parents what a positive affect this trip will have on our educations. We must persuade them that we should ceize this important opportunity. Next, we have to obtain reservations at a youth hostile in Florence. Finely, we have to undergo a through physical examination to make sure we are healthy.

Our conversations about the trip never seem to sease. It is all we can think about! Mr. Duncan advises us to have patients, but we are all counting the days until our departure date.

When our tickets arrive next month, Mr. Duncan will keep them in the school safe so that we do not loose them. I think he believes that our excitement will effect our ability to be responsible. It is a little bit annoying, but we are too happy to be hostel toward him.

I think this is the most exciting thing that has ever happened to me!

Ciao,
Madeline

Building Spelling Skills WEEK 17

Spelling List

This Week's Focus:

- Spell words with the endings **-ent** and **-ant**

STEP 1 Read and Spell	STEP 2 Copy and Spell	STEP 3 Cover and Spell
1. magnificent		
2. obedient		
3. persistent		
4. equivalent		
5. fluorescent		
6. incident		
7. valiant		
8. brilliant		
9. ignorant		
10. significant		
11. reluctant		
12. attendant		
13. dormant		
14. vigilant		
15. radiant		
16. immigrant		
17. accident		
18. confident		
19. ________ bonus word		
20. ________ bonus word		

fold

Word Meaning

Complete the crossword puzzle using spelling words.

Across

1. very bright
3. shining
7. having trust or faith
9. a person who moves from one country to another
10. extremely courageous
11. sleeping; inactive
12. splendid
13. highly watchful
14. a person who takes care of something

Down

2. lacking knowledge
4. showing continuous effort
5. identical in amount
6. important
8. something that happens without being planned

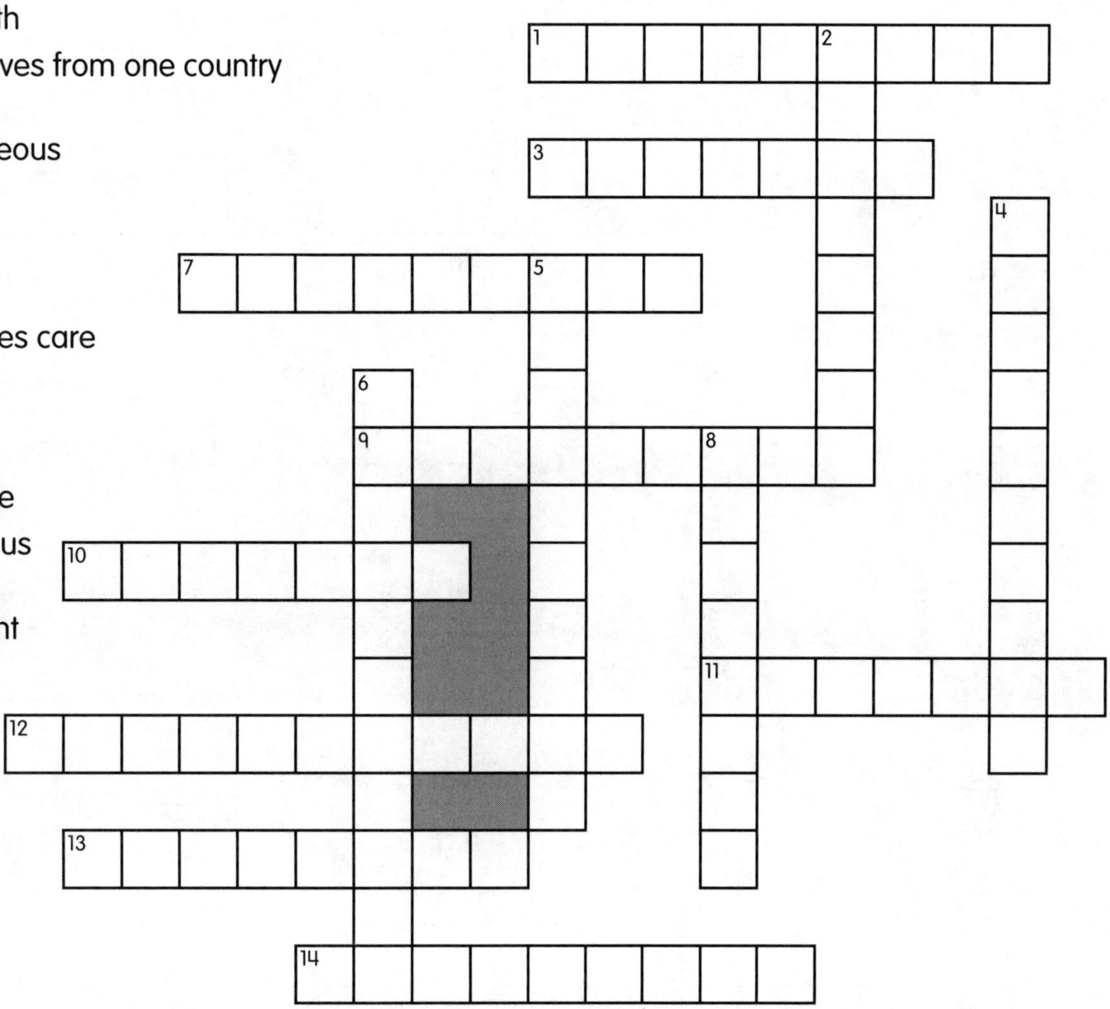

My Spelling Dictation

Write the sentences. Circle the spelling words.

1. ______________________________

____

2. ______________________________

____

Word Study

Match syllables to make spelling words.
Write the complete words on the lines.

1. per	luc	rant	1. persistent
2. con	mi	dant	2. ______
3. fluo	ci	lant	3. ______
4. in	res	ent	4. ______
5. ig	sist	cent	5. ______
6. re	no	tant	6. ______
7. ac	ci	dent	7. ______
8. at	di	dent	8. ______
9. vig	ten	grant	9. ______
10. im	fi	dent	10. ______
11. ra	i	ant	11. ______

12. o	quiv	i	cent	12. ______
13. sig	be	di	lent	13. ______
14. e	nif	i	ent	14. ______
15. mag	nif	a	cant	15. ______

Edit for Spelling

Circle the words that are spelled correctly.

fluorescant	vigalent	confident
valliant	brilliant	obediant
radiant	magnifisent	equivalant
attendent	immigrant	persistent
significant	dorment	reluctent

Circle the misspelled words in the sentences. Write them correctly on the lines.

1. The immigrent children were persistant in their efforts to learn English.

   __________ __________

2. Vanessa was radient after her brilient performance.

   __________ __________

3. The vigillant parking lot attendent was reluctent to give me the keys to my car because I could not find my ticket.

   __________ __________ __________

4. My little brother could not have prevented the acident because he was ignorent of the danger involved in that situation.

   __________ __________

Building Spelling Skills WEEK 18

Spelling List

This Week's Focus:
- Spell words with the /**sh**/ sound

STEP 1 Read and Spell	STEP 2 Copy and Spell	STEP 3 Cover and Spell
1. permission		
2. impatient		
3. dictionary		
4. delicious		
5. ocean		
6. physician		
7. establish		
8. ambitious		
9. surely		
10. magician		
11. conversation		
12. inertia		
13. ashes		
14. official		
15. sufficient		
16. glacier		
17. brochure		
18. friendship		
19. ________ bonus word		
20. ________ bonus word		

(fold)

Word Meaning

Fill in the blanks with spelling words.

1. During their ____________________, Joanne's ____________________ asked her if she was eating a ____________________ amount of vegetables.

2. We ate at a restaurant in Maryland that served ____________________ crabs fresh from the ____________________.

3. "Please hurry up and clean the ____________________ out of the fireplace!" said Grandmother in an ____________________ tone.

4. The ____________________ was an ____________________ young woman who wanted to ____________________ herself as the top performer of the year.

5. ____________________ this attractive and informative ____________________ will encourage many people to visit the museum.

6. The reporter asked ____________________ for a ____________________ with the politician.

My Spelling Dictation

Write the sentences. Circle the spelling words.

1. ____

____

2. ____

____

Word Study

Circle the letter or letters in each word that make the /**sh**/ sound.

1. permission
2. establish
3. inertia
4. brochure
5. dictionary
6. magician
7. ocean
8. surely

How many different ways is the /**sh**/ sound spelled? ________

Fill in the missing syllables to make spelling words.

1. deli________
2. estab________
3. impa________
4. of________cial
5. o________
6. bro________
7. permis________
8. magi________
9. ________bitious
10. conversa________
11. gla________
12. iner________
13. ________ficient
14. physi________
15. dic________ary
16. ________ship

Edit for Spelling

Circle the word in each row that is spelled correctly.

1. freindship	frienship	friendship
2. ambishous	ambitious	ambicious
3. official	oficial	offisial
4. glacier	glashure	glasier
5. magitian	magician	maggician
6. impasient	impateint	impatient
7. shurly	shurely	surely
8. estabblish	establish	establich
9. ocaen	occean	ocean
10. conversashun	conversation	conversacion
11. delicious	delishous	dilicious
12. brochoor	broshure	brochure

Circle the misspelled words in the sentences. Write them correctly on the lines.

1. I would like to have a serious conversasion with Marie about our freindship.

   ____________________ ____________________

2. The magisian got permiscion from his physition before he performed the difficult trick.

   ____________________ ____________________ ____________________

3. From the deck of the cruise ship, we watched a large chunk of the glasier fall into the ocian.

   ____________________ ____________________

Building Spelling Skills WEEK 19

Spelling List

This Week's Focus:

- Spell words with the suffixes **-able**, **-ible**, and **-ous**

STEP 1 Read and Spell	STEP 2 Copy and Spell	STEP 3 Cover and Spell
1. audible		
2. plausible		
3. indelible		
4. compatible		
5. credible		
6. sensible		
7. profitable		
8. durable		
9. lovable		
10. acceptable		
11. predictable		
12. changeable		
13. infectious		
14. curious		
15. cautious		
16. precious		
17. vicious		
18. numerous		
19. ______ bonus word		
20. ______ bonus word		

fold

Word Meaning

Match each word to its meaning. Write the letter on the line.

_____ 1. audible	a. long lasting
_____ 2. plausible	b. able to be heard
_____ 3. indelible	c. valuable
_____ 4. compatible	d. cruel; mean
_____ 5. credible	e. many in number
_____ 6. infectious	f. careful
_____ 7. numerous	g. believable
_____ 8. vicious	h. easy to foretell
_____ 9. precious	i. easily spread or caught
_____ 10. cautious	j. trustworthy
_____ 11. predictable	k. able to get along together
_____ 12. durable	l. permanent; unable to be removed or washed away

My Spelling Dictation

Write the sentences. Circle the spelling words.

1. ____

____

2. ____

____

Word Study

Fill in the blanks with the missing vowel.

1. indel___ble
2. sens___ble
3. predict___ble
4. aud___ble
5. lov___ble
6. plaus___ble
7. accept___ble
8. compat___ble
9. profit___ble
10. dur___ble

Divide these words into syllables.
Write the syllables on the lines.

1. cautious ______________________
2. curious ______________________
3. numerous ______________________
4. audible ______________________
5. credible ______________________
6. infectious ______________________
7. sensible ______________________
8. compatible ______________________
9. predictable ______________________
10. profitable ______________________

Edit for Spelling

Circle the words that are spelled correctly.

acceptible	precious	numerous
changable	compatable	sensable
infectious	indelable	durible
viscious	audible	lovable
curious	predictible	credible

Circle the misspelled words in the sentences.
Write them correctly on the lines.

1. Eleanor was currious about the profitible business opportunity.

   ____________________ ____________________

2. Rob made a sensable decision and bought the most durible jacket he could find.

   ____________________ ____________________

3. I am very causious when I am driving with my presious children in the car.

   ____________________ ____________________

4. Paul was upset when he discovered nummerous indelable marks on the back of his shirt.

   ____________________ ____________________

Building Spelling Skills WEEK 20

Spelling List

This Week's Focus:
- Spell plural forms of words

STEP 1 Read and Spell	STEP 2 Copy and Spell	STEP 3 Cover and Spell
1. mosquitoes		
2. varieties		
3. beliefs		
4. grievances		
5. schedules		
6. echoes		
7. thieves		
8. journeys		
9. halves		
10. passersby		
11. substances		
12. orchestras		
13. pharmacies		
14. sergeants		
15. tomatoes		
16. boundaries		
17. instruments		
18. encyclopedias		
19. ________ bonus word		
20. ________ bonus word		

fold

Word Meaning

Complete the crossword puzzle using spelling words.

Across

1. things that are regarded as true
3. small biting insects
5. complaints
6. red fruits, usually eaten as vegetables
8. borders
10. reflected sounds
13. kinds
14. devices used to do particular things
15. trips

Down

2. lists showing the times at which events will occur
4. collections of information about many branches of knowledge
7. drugstores
9. materials
11. people who pass by
12. the two equal parts of something

My Spelling Dictation

Write the sentences. Circle the spelling words.

1. ______________________________

____

2. ______________________________

____

Word Study

Change each singular noun to its plural form.
Check the box that shows how you changed the word.

		add **s** or **es**	change **y** to **i** and add **es**	change **f** to **v** and add **es**
1. half	______			
2. orchestra	______			
3. instrument	______			
4. variety	______			
5. thief	______			
6. sergeant	______			
7. boundary	______			
8. pharmacy	______			
9. echo	______			
10. journey	______			
11. substance	______			
12. tomato	______			
13. belief	______			
14. mosquito	______			
15. encyclopedia	______			
16. schedule	______			
17. grievance	______			

Edit for Spelling

Circle the misspelled words in the sentences.
Write them correctly on the lines.

1. The directors of all the orchestraes in the region gathered at a conference.

2. No pharmacys are likely to be open at this time of night.

3. Several good encyclopeedias are available on the Internet.

4. The surveyors used their instrumants to measure the bounderies of the property.

5. On several of our journies down the river, the mosquitos have been very bothersome.

6. All of the employees at our company filed grievences about our sckedules.

7. My assignment for the school paper was to ask passerbys about their believes regarding life on other planets.

8. The theives stole several varietes of tommatoes from the garden.

Building Spelling Skills WEEK 21

Spelling List

This Week's Focus:

- Spell words with the suffixes **-ment**, **-ful**, and **-less**

STEP 1 Read and Spell	STEP 2 Copy and Spell	STEP 3 Cover and Spell
1. government		
2. judgment		
3. experiment		
4. development		
5. amazement		
6. enjoyment		
7. painless		
8. tireless		
9. humorless		
10. effortless		
11. powerless		
12. colorless		
13. successful		
14. doubtful		
15. cheerful		
16. careful		
17. grateful		
18. thoughtful		
19. ______ bonus word		
20. ______ bonus word		

fold

Word Meaning

Complete these tasks using spelling words.

1. Write the word that means without...

   a. power ______________________ d. fatigue ______________________

   b. color ______________________ e. pain ______________________

   c. humor ______________________

2. Write the word that describes how a person might feel...

   a. when she is given information that seems unlikely to be true ______________________

   b. when he is happy ______________________

3. Match each word to its meaning. Write the letter on the line.

________	experiment	a. the process of ruling a country or state
________	development	b. considerate
________	government	c. the ability to decide or evaluate
________	judgment	d. having success
________	enjoyment	e. a test to prove or discover something
________	thoughtful	f. the action of enjoying something
________	successful	g. something that has happened

My Spelling Dictation

Write the sentences. Circle the spelling words.

1. ____

____

2. ____

____

Word Study

Add the correct suffix to the base word.

1. The dentist made the procedure as ________________ (pain) as possible.
2. We all stared in ________________ (amaze) at the magician's tricks.
3. My brother showed good ________________ (judge) when he chose that dependable car.
4. Everyone loves Judy because she is such a ________________ (thought) person.
5. The dancer's moves seemed ________________ (effort) as she floated across the stage.
6. Carl rushed to the phone to report the latest ________________ (develop) in the story he was covering.

Divide these words into syllables.
Write the syllables on the lines. Then circle the suffix.

1. government ________________________________
2. successful ________________________________
3. humorless ________________________________
4. enjoyment ________________________________
5. effortless ________________________________
6. amazement ________________________________

Edit for Spelling

Circle the words that have the correct suffix.

successment	tireful	grateful
doubtment	amazeless	developless
judgment	humorful	enjoyment
thoughtment	experiment	effortment
carement	colorless	painment

Circle the misspelled words in the sentences.
Write them correctly on the lines.

1. American democracy was a new experriment in goverment.

   ____________________ ____________________

2. The gloomy, collorless sky did not make me feel very cheerfull.

   ____________________ ____________________

3. Betty showed her doutful family that she could indeed be sucessful in her new job.

   ____________________ ____________________

4. We were greatful that the movers were carefull with our belongings and made the packing seem so efortless.

   ____________________ ____________________ ____________________

Building **Spelling** Skills WEEK 22

Spelling List

This Week's Focus:

- Spell words with the prefixes **un-**, **im-**, **in-**, and **under-**
- Practice adding prefixes to base words

STEP 1 Read and Spell	STEP 2 Copy and Spell	STEP 3 Cover and Spell
1. immature		
2. immobile		
3. imperfect		
4. immortal		
5. immediate		
6. unsure		
7. unlikely		
8. unreliable		
9. uncertain		
10. inability		
11. inanimate		
12. incautious		
13. independent		
14. inconvenient		
15. underneath		
16. undercover		
17. underage		
18. underestimate		
19. ______ bonus word		
20. ______ bonus word		

fold

Word Meaning

Fill in the blanks with spelling words.

1. The information in that newspaper is often ____________________.

2. Mom says it is ____________________ that Bill will change jobs in the ____________________ future.

3. Even though Mallory is almost ____________________ due to a body cast, she is trying to be ____________________ and do everything for herself.

4. Don't ____________________ those capable young people just because they are still somewhat ____________________.

5. The ____________________ of the object to move means that it is ____________________.

6. It is a fact of life that all human beings are ____________________.

7. The daring boy made an ____________________ leap from the roof of the garage.

8. It is ____________________ whether the ____________________ spy revealed his true identity.

My Spelling Dictation

Write the sentences. Circle the spelling words.

1. ____

____

2. ____

____

Word Study

Add the correct prefix that means "not" to each base word. Write **un**, **in**, or **im**.

1. ______likely
2. ______cautious
3. ______convenient
4. ______mortal
5. ______mobile
6. ______sure
7. ______mature
8. ______reliable
9. ______dependent
10. ______ability

Write the spelling word that is an antonym for each word.

1. careful ____________
2. over ____________
3. convenient ____________
4. overestimate ____________
5. delayed ____________
6. dependable ____________
7. perfect ____________
8. full-grown ____________
9. ability ____________
10. certain ____________
11. sure ____________
12. mobile ____________
13. mortal ____________
14. animate ____________

Edit for Spelling

Circle the words that have the correct prefix.

inlikely	inability	inconvenient
unmediate	uncertain	unanimate
imdependent	imreliable	immature
unsure	inperfect	imcautious

Circle the misspelled words in the sentences.
Write them on the lines correctly.

1. It is unlikly that the unrealiable evidence will be used in the trial.

   ____________________ ____________________

2. The detective was unsertain about the success of his undercuver assignment.

   ____________________ ____________________

3. Rose was unshure what was making the rattling noise underneeth her car.

   ____________________ ____________________

4. I don't want to underestimait the amount of food I will need for the party.

   ____

5. The imiture little bear was too independant and incawtious for his own good.

   ____________________ ____________________ ____________________

Building WEEK 23 **Spelling** Skills

Spelling List

This Week's Focus:

- Spell words with **geo**, **act**, **bio**, **port**, and **graph**

STEP 1 Read and Spell	STEP 2 Copy and Spell	STEP 3 Cover and Spell
1. geology		
2. geography		
3. geologist		
4. graphite		
5. autograph		
6. photograph		
7. biopsy		
8. biology		
9. biography		
10. biosphere		
11. transact		
12. enact		
13. actor		
14. react		
15. import		
16. transport		
17. portable		
18. export		
19. ________ bonus word		
20. ________ bonus word		

fold

Word Meaning

Fill in the blanks with spelling words.

1. Shannon asked the famous ____________ to ____________ his ____________.

2. Jim took several ____________ classes to learn about the formation of the earth and to help him decide if he wanted to be a ____________.

3. Some countries ____________ their extra food and ____________ items that they cannot produce for themselves.

4. ____________ is my favorite subject in school because I love to look at maps and learn about other countries.

5. We will have to arrange for a truck to ____________ this shipment of ____________ to the pencil factory.

6. My sister studied ____________ to learn about living things before she went to medical school.

7. I read a terrific ____________ about the life of Thomas Jefferson.

My Spelling Dictation

Write the sentences. Circle the spelling words.

1. ____

____

2. ____

____

Word Study

Use these words to help you answer the questions below.

bio = life	**auto** = self
port = carry	**trans** = across
geo = earth	**im** = into
act = do	**graph** = write

ology = study of

ist = one who studies

or = one who

What word parts make words meaning...?

1. "one who does"

   ________ + ________ = ____________

2. "carry across"

   ________ + ________ = ____________

3. "written story about a life"

   ________ + ________ + y = ____________

4. "write about the world"

   ________ + ________ + y = ____________

5. "the study of life"

   ________ + ________ = ____________

6. "carry into"

   ________ + ________ = ____________

7. "one who studies the earth"
   (This is a hard one; you have to leave out some letters.)

   ________ + ________ + ________ = ____________

Edit for Spelling

Circle the word in each row that is spelled correctly.

1. transact	trannsact	transactt
2. autogragh	autigraph	autograph
3. gelogy	geollogy	geology
4. biospear	biosphere	biosfere
5. transpoart	transport	trannsport
6. geography	geogerphy	goegraphy
7. grafite	graffite	graphite
8. fotograph	photograph	photagraph
9. biopsy	biopsey	byopsie
10. biogerphy	biography	biograffy
11. inact	ennact	enact
12. acter	acctor	actor
13. import	immport	emport
14. portible	portable	poartable
15. export	exsport	exportt
16. bilogy	biology	bialogy

Building WEEK 24
Spelling
Skills

Spelling List

This Week's Focus:
- Spell words for **said**

STEP 1 Read and Spell	STEP 2 Copy and Spell	STEP 3 Cover and Spell
1. admitted		
2. answered		
3. concluded		
4. exclaimed		
5. insisted		
6. remarked		
7. whispered		
8. advised		
9. blurted		
10. commented		
11. demanded		
12. explained		
13. mentioned		
14. observed		
15. replied		
16. whined		
17. screamed		
18. inquired		
19. ______ bonus word		
20. ______ bonus word		

(fold)

Word Meaning

Fill in the blanks with spelling words.

1. The guilty boy finally ______________ that he had taken the money.
2. The tired puppy ______________ and whimpered until it fell asleep.
3. The frightened girl ______________ for help.
4. I accidentally ______________ out the answer.
5. When the teacher questioned Richard, he ______________ correctly.
6. My boss ______________ that I get to work on time.
7. Dad patiently ______________ the reasons for his decision.
8. I ______________ softly to my friend during the movie.
9. Jane stubbornly ______________ on having her own way at all times.
10. My counselor ______________ me to study hard for the big test.
11. Chris casually ______________ what he would like for his birthday.

My Spelling Dictation

Write the sentences. Circle the spelling words.

1. ____

____

2. ____

____

Word Study

Add the ending **ed** to each word.
Write the new word on the line. Check the rule you used for each word.

	No change	double the last consonant	change **y** to **i**	drop the silent **e**
1. admit ____________				
2. demand ____________				
3. reply ____________				
4. whine ____________				
5. insist ____________				
6. advise ____________				
7. observe ____________				
8. scream ____________				

Count the syllables in each word. Write the number on the line.

1. replied ______
2. screamed ______
3. mentioned ______
4. commented ______
5. answered ______
6. whined ______
7. inquired ______
8. insisted ______
9. explained ______
10. concluded ______
11. remarked ______
12. whispered ______
13. advised ______
14. blurted ______
15. demanded ______
16. observed ______

Edit for Spelling

Circle the 15 misspelled words below.
Write the words correctly on the lines.

Baby-sitting Blues

"Have you ever had a terrible baby-sitting experience?" Carol inquiered.

"Oh, yes," I repplied. "Last week, I took care of two children who wined and screemed all day long. Their mother had menshuned that they were not feeling well, but I insissted that I could handle the job. What a mistake!"

"How awful," exclamed Carol. "What did you do?"

"Well, first I explaned that they would feel better if they would calm down," I remarcked. "Then, I demandded that they both take naps."

"I've observd your child-care skills," comented Carol. "I'm sure you were able to comfort the children."

"Yes," I admited. "I wispered stories to them until they fell asleep. When they woke up, they were much happier."

"Well," Carol conclooded, "I don't think baby-sitting is the job for me!"

______	______	______
______	______	______
______	______	______
______	______	______
______	______	______

Building **Spelling** Skills WEEK 25

Spelling List

This Week's Focus:

- Spell words with the suffixes **-ship** and **-ancy**
- Spell words with the endings **-ly** and **-en**

STEP 1 Read and Spell	STEP 2 Copy and Spell	STEP 3 Cover and Spell
1. especially		
2. immediately		
3. permanently		
4. temporarily		
5. perfectly		
6. sincerely		
7. buoyancy		
8. truancy		
9. vacancy		
10. citizenship		
11. partnership		
12. ownership		
13. championship		
14. membership		
15. strengthen		
16. lengthen		
17. frighten		
18. fasten		
19. ________ bonus word		
20. ________ bonus word		

fold

Word Meaning

Complete the crossword puzzle using spelling words.

Across
1. in a way that is not permanent
5. in a way that is lasting
7. the ability to float
9. to make stronger
11. to scare
13. to make longer
14. the state of being a citizen

Down
2. particularly
3. a formal relationship of sharing
4. absence from school without permission
6. without delay
8. the state of possessing something
10. flawlessly
11. to hold together

My Spelling Dictation

Write the sentences. Circle the spelling words.

1. ______________________________

____

2. ______________________________

____

Word Study

Add the suffix or ending to each word. You may need to make some spelling changes.

ly

1. immediate ______________________
2. permanent ______________________
3. temporary ______________________

ancy

4. truant ______________________
5. vacant ______________________
6. buoyant ______________________

ship

7. citizen ______________________
8. champion ______________________
9. owner ______________________

en

10. length ______________________
11. strength ______________________
12. fright ______________________

Write the base word. You may need to add some letters to make several of the base words.

1. sincerely ______________________
2. lengthen ______________________
3. membership ______________________
4. permanently ______________________
5. vacancy ______________________
6. partnership ______________________
7. frighten ______________________
8. buoyancy ______________________
9. truancy ______________________
10. temporarily ______________________
11. perfectly ______________________

Edit for Spelling

Circle the words that are spelled correctly.

temperarily	membership	fassen
ownership	vacantcy	perminently
espeshally	frightten	sinserely
buoyancy	truancy	immediately
strenthen	champeenship	perfictly

Circle the misspelled words.
Write them correctly on the lines.

1. Mrs. Gomez sinserely wants to obtain her citizanship.

   __________________ __________________

2. My piano teacher was espescially happy with me because I performed purfectly at the recital.

   __________________ __________________

3. The vacuncy at the hotel will probably be filled immidiately.

   __________________ __________________

4. Joe's mimbership on the team will strengten our chances to win the champpionship.

   __________________ __________________ __________________

Building Spelling Skills WEEK 26

Spelling List

This Week's Focus:

- Spell words with the prefixes **mis-**, **dis-**, **re-**, **non-**, and **anti-**
- Practice adding prefixes to base words

STEP 1 Read and Spell	STEP 2 Copy and Spell	STEP 3 Cover and Spell
1. misspell	______	______
2. misbehave	______	______
3. misfortune	______	______
4. misdirect	______	______
5. dishonest	______	______
6. discourage	______	______
7. disagree	______	______
8. disgrace	______	______
9. antisocial	______	______
10. antifreeze	______	______
11. antiseptic	______	______
12. reappear	______	______
13. rewrite	______	______
14. recede	______	______
15. nonsense	______	______
16. nonconformist	______	______
17. nonexistent	______	______
18. nonfiction	______	______
19. ______ bonus word	______	______
20. ______ bonus word	______	______

(fold)

Word Meaning

Complete these tasks using spelling words.

1. Write the spelling word that means…

   a. a person who does not think or behave like the majority ______________________

   b. writing that presents or discusses facts ______________________

   c. to spell incorrectly ______________________

   d. unfriendly ______________________

   e. bad luck ______________________

   f. to move back ______________________

2. Read the word. Then write the meaning for its prefix.

   a. misbehave: **mis** means... ______________________

   b. reappear: **re** means... ______________________

   c. antifreeze: **anti** means... ______________________

   d. nonexistent: **non** means... ______________________

My Spelling Dictation

Write the sentences. Circle the spelling words.

1. ____

   ____

2. ____

   ____

Word Study

Add the correct prefix to the base word.

mis	dis	anti	re	non

1. Eric made a silly comment, and Dad told him to stop talking ______________. (sense)

2. After Ruthie helped me edit my first draft, I was eager to ______________ (write) my paper.

3. Unfortunately, the man we elected to office turned out to be ______________ (honest) and untrustworthy.

4. Fred and I ______________ (agree) about many things, but we are still good friends.

5. The school nurse washed the cut on my knee with ______________ (septic) soap.

6. Randy vowed that he would never cheat on a test because it would be too big a ______________. (grace)

7. Coach Brody told us not to let the score ______________ (courage) us from playing our best.

Add a prefix to make each word into its opposite.

1. spell ______________
2. fiction ______________
4. appear ______________
5. direct ______________

Edit for Spelling

Circle the words that have the correct prefix.

misfortune	disbehave	refiction
dissense	antihonest	nonexistent
recourage	disgrace	discourage
antifortune	nonwrite	recede

Circle the misspelled words in the sentences.
Write them correctly on the lines.

1. Granddad put antifreaze in his new sports car.

 ____

2. Please do not misbahave on the field trip and desgrace our school.

 ______________ ______________

3. I believe that ghosts are inexistant, but some people misagree.

 ______________ ______________

4. Alexandra is a disconformist, but she is not disonnest.

 ______________ ______________

5. It was my mysfortune to mispell the word "antiseptick" in the spelling contest.

 ______________ ______________ ______________

Building Spelling Skills WEEK 27

Spelling List

This Week's Focus:
- Spell adjectives

STEP 1 Read and Spell | **STEP 2 Copy and Spell** | **STEP 3 Cover and Spell**

fold

1. punctual
2. ancient
3. miniature
4. stupendous
5. inquisitive
6. wasteful
7. zealous
8. obnoxious
9. pathetic
10. obsolete
11. ridiculous
12. genuine
13. congenial
14. optimistic
15. reliable
16. abundant
17. meager
18. sparse
19. ______ bonus word
20. ______ bonus word

Word Meaning

Write the spelling word that means...

1. more than enough ______
2. very old ______
3. able to depend on ______
4. silly ______
5. real; authentic ______
6. on time ______
7. tiny ______
8. full of questions ______
9. wonderful ______
10. nice; gets along with others ______
11. offensive or not pleasant ______
12. causing feelings of pity ______
13. hopeful that things will go well ______
14. no longer in use ______

My Spelling Dictation

Write the sentences. Circle the spelling words.

1. ______

______

2. ______

______

Word Study

Write the spelling words that are synonyms of these words.

1. hopeful ____________
2. real ____________
3. dependable ____________
4. curious ____________
5. pitiful ____________
6. absurd ____________
7. scarce ____________
8. enthusiastic ____________
9. unthrifty ____________
10. outdated ____________
11. prompt ____________
12. friendly ____________
13. plentiful ____________
14. tremendous ____________

Write the spelling words that are synonyms of the words in parentheses.

1. It is ____________ (absurd) how quickly my computer became ____________ (outdated).
2. Our food supply is ____________ (insufficient), so we cannot be ____________ (unthrifty).
3. My car may be ____________ (old) but it is still very ____________ (dependable).
4. Her ____________ (friendly) nature shows in her ____________ (real) enjoyment of others.

Edit for Spelling

Circle the 11 misspelled words below.
Write the words correctly on the lines.

The Birthday Present

For my birthday, my parents gave me the most stoopendous present ever! It is the cutest miniture poodle puppy you have ever seen. I named her Poppy. She is inkwisitive and playful and lots of fun.

Our ancsient cat, Oscar, thinks Poppy is rediculous. It is obvious that Poppy's antics are obnoxshus to him. Poppy tries to be congeenial, but Oscar just puts his nose in the air and walks away. I am optamistic that in time the two of them will become ginuine friends. In the meantime, it is pethetic to see Oscar looking so unhappy. He probably feels that he is obsalete, now that we have a new pet.

Building **Spelling** Skills

WEEK 28

Spelling List

This Week's Focus:

- Spell words with the prefixes **bi-**, **tri-**, **uni-**, **semi-**, and **cent-**

STEP 1 Read and Spell | STEP 2 Copy and Spell | STEP 3 Cover and Spell

fold

1. binocular
2. bicentennial
3. bilingual
4. bipedal
5. triceps
6. triathlon
7. triad
8. triplicate
9. unicorn
10. unify
11. union
12. unique
13. semicircle
14. semicolon
15. semiannual
16. centipede
17. century
18. centennial
19. ______ bonus word
20. ______ bonus word

Word Meaning

Match each word to its meaning. Write the letter on the line.

____	1. semiannual	a. in sets of 3
____	2. centipede	b. half a circle
____	3. bilingual	c. having two feet
____	4. triad	d. employing both eyes
____	5. unify	e. unlike any other; being the only one
____	6. centennial	f. a creature with many pairs of legs (literally "hundred legs")
____	7. bipedal	g. twice a year
____	8. triathlon	h. to bring together as one
____	9. unique	i. speaking two languages
____	10. triplicate	j. a group of three
____	11. semicircle	k. a 100th anniversary
____	12. binocular	l. a three-part athletic event

My Spelling Dictation

Write the sentences. Circle the spelling words.

1. ____

____

2. ____

____

Word Study

Each of the words in the box begins with a prefix that has a numerical meaning.

Write each word from the box on the line beneath the meaning of its prefix. Use a dictionary to find at least one more word to add to each list.

union	century	semicolon	bipedal	unicorn
bilingual	unify	centipede	triathlon	semiannual
centennial	triceps	triad	binocular	
semicircle	unique	bicentennial	triplicate	

half

____
____
____
____
____

one

____
____
____
____
____

two

____
____
____
____
____

three

____
____
____
____
____

one hundred

____
____
____
____
____

Edit for Spelling

Circle the word in each row that is spelled correctly.

1.	uniffy	unafy	unify
2.	centipede	sentipede	centipeed
3.	semicirkle	semicircle	cemicircle
4.	billingual	bilingual	bylingual
5.	cintury	century	sentury
6.	bipedal	bipeedal	bipiedal
7.	unnicorn	unicorrn	unicorn
8.	benocular	bioculer	binocular
9.	tirad	triad	triadd
10.	unique	uniquee	unnique

Circle the misspelled words in the sentences. Write them correctly on the lines.

1. Our community is hosting a triathalon to celebrate our bicentenial.

   ______________________ ______________________

2. The kindhearted unnicorn began to cry when it stepped on a centapede.

   ______________________ ______________________

3. In this centery it will be important to be bilinguil.

   ______________________ ______________________

4. The secretary filled out the forms in triplecate and made sure that each semicollon was in its proper place.

   ______________________ ______________________

Building **Spelling** Skills

WEEK 29

Spelling List

This Week's Focus:

- Spell words with **rupt**, **spec**, **sign**, **scope**, and **form**

STEP 1 Read and Spell | **STEP 2** Copy and Spell | **STEP 3** Cover and Spell

fold

1. eruption
2. interrupt
3. bankrupt
4. rupture
5. spectator
6. suspect
7. respect
8. spectacle
9. signature
10. insignia
11. signal
12. microscope
13. telescope
14. stethoscope
15. uniform
16. reformat
17. formal
18. transform
19. ______ bonus word
20. ______ bonus word

Word Meaning

Fill in the blanks using spelling words.

1. The king wrote his ____________________ at the bottom of the decree.

2. At the hospital, the doctor listened to my heart with a ____________________, and then looked at some of my blood through a ____________________.

3. Each student is required to wear a ____________________.

4. I was thrilled to be a ____________________ at the recent ____________________ of Mount Kilauea.

5. I ____________________ that Lydia will soon be ____________________ because she is spending money so carelessly.

6. Please try not to ____________________ Dr. Boyer when he is looking through the ____________________ at the stars.

7. Have you ever watched a caterpillar ____________________ itself into a beautiful butterfly?

8. The movie stars in their ____________________ clothes are quite a ____________________.

My Spelling Dictation

Write the sentences. Circle the spelling words.

1. ____

____

2. ____

____

Word Study

Use these word parts to help you answer the questions below.

uni = one	**micro** = small	**rupt** = break	**scope** = view
inter = between	**trans** = change	**form** = shape	

What word parts make words meaning…?

1. "to break between"

   ________ + ________ = ____________

2. "clothes in one shape or style"

   ________ + ________ = ____________

3. "used to view small things"

   ________ + ________ = ____________

4. "to change shape"

   ________ + ________ = ____________

Count the syllables in each word. Write the number on the line.

1. stethoscope ________
2. reformat ________
3. uniform ________
4. respect ________
5. insignia ________
6. rupture ________
7. bankrupt ________
8. telescope ________
9. suspect ________
10. signature ________
11. spectacle ________
12. signal ________
13. interrupt ________
14. eruption ________
15. formal ________
16. spectator ________

Edit for Spelling

Circle the 9 misspelled words below.
Write them correctly on the lines below.

The Rupture

Nurse Callaway put on her uneform and rode her bicycle to her job at the school. When she arrived in the office, Rudy was already there, holding his side and groaning. Nurse Callaway adjusted her specktacles and placed her stethascope around her neck, and then called Rudy into the examining room.

Rudy was one of Nurse Callaway's favorite students. He had managed to transsform his behavior over the past few months. Instead of being sullen and angry, Rudy was now full of fun. He liked to play friendly jokes on everyone and could be counted on to interupt a dull class with an amusing comment. Rudy had won the resppect of the staff for his hard work and cheerful nature.

All the same, Nurse Callaway susspected that Rudy was not really ill. She thought he was pretending to be sick so that he could have a chance to look through her micrascope. After a short examination, she quickly changed her mind.

"Oh, Rudy," she exclaimed. "I believe you are suffering from a rupchured appendix!"

Building Spelling Skills WEEK 30

Spelling List

This Week's Focus:
- Spell content vocabulary words

STEP 1 Read and Spell	STEP 2 Copy and Spell	STEP 3 Cover and Spell
1. environment		
2. Antarctica		
3. international		
4. peninsula		
5. constitutional		
6. bureaucracy		
7. patriotism		
8. hemisphere		
9. archeology		
10. atmospheric		
11. cartographer		
12. coordinates		
13. parallelogram		
14. perpendicular		
15. rhombus		
16. theorem		
17. polyhedron		
18. circumference		
19. ______ bonus word		
20. ______ bonus word		

fold

Word Meaning

Answer the questions using spelling words.

1. What do you call someone who makes maps? ____________________

2. Which words describe two-dimensional figures? ____________________

____

3. Which word names a continent? ____________________

Where is this continent located? Southern ____________________

4. Which word means "the study of ancient relics and cultures"? ____________________

5. Which word names a landform? ____________________

6. Which word means "the outside of a circle"? ____________________

7. Which word means "having to do with two or more countries"? ____________________

8. Which word means "the entire natural world"? ____________________

My Spelling Dictation

Write the sentences. Circle the spelling words.

1. ____

____

2. ____

____

Word Study

The words in the box are words you might hear in some of your classes.

Write each word under the subject in which you would be most likely to use it. Some words may fit in more than one category.

theorem	constitutional	peninsula	patriotism
Antarctica	atmospheric	bureaucracy	hemisphere
rhombus	perpendicular	environment	coordinates

Mathematics

____

____

____

____

Geography

____

____

____

____

Government

____

____

____

____

Science

____

____

____

____

Edit for Spelling

Circle the words that are spelled correctly.

archiology	sircumference	penninsula
international	parallelogram	patriottism
Antarctica	burochracy	atmospheric
rhombas	polyhedron	envirnment
cordinates	hemisfere	perpendicular

Circle the misspelled words in the sentences.
Write them correctly on the lines.

1. The cartogerpher carefully measured the circumfrence of the lake.

   ____________________ ____________________

2. The envirenment in antartica is extremely cold and icy.

   ____________________ ____________________

3. In a paralelogram no line is perpindicular to another.

   ____________________ ____________________

4. The internationel group of explorers traveled around the penensula for several weeks.

   ____________________ ____________________

Note: Use this form to track students' spelling progress.

Spelling Record Sheet

Building Spelling Skills

Students' Names																	
1																	
2																	
3																	
4																	
5																	
6																	
7																	
8																	
9																	
10																	
11																	
12																	
13																	
14																	
15																	
16																	
17																	
18																	
19																	
20																	
21																	
22																	
23																	
24																	
25																	
26																	
27																	
28																	
29																	
30																	

Note: Reproduce this form twice for each student to track his or her progress.

My Spelling Record

Building Spelling Skills

Spelling List	Date	Number Correct	Words Missed

Note: Reproduce this form for the end-of-the-week test.

Spelling Test

Building Spelling Skills

Listen to the words.
Write each word on a line.

1. ______________ 11. ______________
2. ______________ 12. ______________
3. ______________ 13. ______________
4. ______________ 14. ______________
5. ______________ 15. ______________
6. ______________ 16. ______________
7. ______________ 17. ______________
8. ______________ 18. ______________
9. ______________ 19. ______________
10. ______________ 20. ______________

Listen to the sentences.
Write them on the lines.

1. ______________________________

____

____

2. ______________________________

____

____

Building **Spelling** Skills

Spelling List

Note: Reproduce this form to make your own spelling list.

STEP 1 Read and Spell	STEP 2 Copy and Spell	STEP 3 Cover and Spell
1. ________	________	________
2. ________	________	________
3. ________	________	________
4. ________	________	________
5. ________	________	________
6. ________	________	________
7. ________	________	________
8. ________	________	________
9. ________	________	________
10. ________	________	________
11. ________	________	________
12. ________	________	________
13. ________	________	________
14. ________	________	________
15. ________	________	________
16. ________	________	________
17. ________	________	________
18. ________	________	________
19. ________	________	________
20. ________	________	________

fold

Note: Reproduce this form to make your own crossword puzzles.

Crossword Puzzle

Across	Down

Note: Reproduce this letter to send home with spelling lists.

Building Spelling Skills

Dear Parents,

Attached is your child's spelling list for this week. Encourage him or her to practice the words in one or more of these ways:

1. Read and spell each word. Cover it up and write it. Uncover the word and check to see if it is correct.
2. Find the words on the spelling list in printed materials such as books and magazines.
3. Read a word aloud and ask your child to spell it (either aloud or written on paper).

Thank you for your support of our spelling program.

Sincerely,

Building Spelling Skills

Dear Parents,

Attached is your child's spelling list for this week. Encourage him or her to practice the words in one or more of these ways:

1. Read and spell each word. Cover it up and write it. Uncover the word and check to see if it is correct.
2. Find the words on the spelling list in printed materials such as books and magazines.
3. Read a word aloud and ask your child to spell it (either aloud or written on paper).

Thank you for your support of our spelling program.

Sincerely,

Student Spelling Dictionaries

Self-made spelling dictionaries provide students with a reference for the spelling of words they frequently use in their writing.

Materials

- copy of "My Own Spelling Dictionary" form (page 147)
- 26 sheets of lined paper—6" x 9" (15 x 23 cm)
- 2 sheets of construction paper or tagboard for cover—6" x 9" (15 x 23 cm)
- crayons or markers
- glue
- stapler
- masking tape

Steps to Follow

1. Color and cut out the cover sheet form. Glue it to the front cover of the dictionary.

2. Staple the lined paper inside the cover. Place masking tape over the staples.

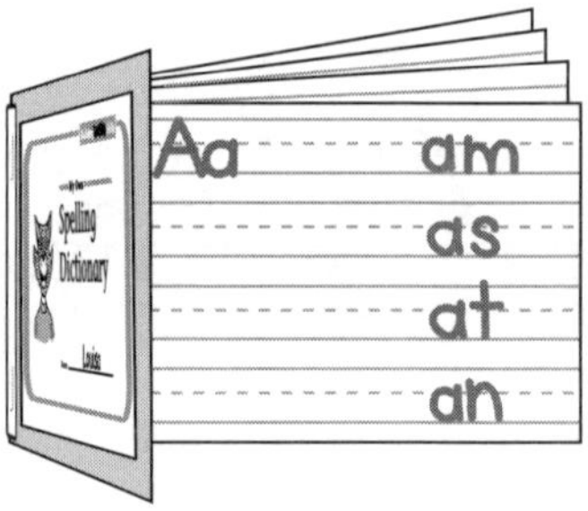

3. Guide students (or ask parent volunteers) to write a letter of the alphabet on each page.

What to Include

1. When students ask for the correct spelling of a special word, have them write it in their dictionary.
2. Include special words being learned as part of science or social studies units.
3. Include words for special holidays.
4. Include the common words students continue to misspell on tests and in daily written work.

Building Spelling Skills

My Own

Spelling Dictionary

Name ______________________________

Building Spelling Skills

My Own

Spelling Dictionary

Name ______________________________

Master Word List

abbreviate
absent-minded
absolutely
abundant
acceptable
accident
achievement
acknowledge
acquire
acre
action
actor
admitted
advised
affect
agent
algebra
all ready
alliance
already
although
amazement
ambition
ambitious
amphibian
ancient
angrier
angriest
answered
Antarctica
antelope
antenna
anticipate
antifreeze
antiseptic
antisocial
anywhere
appearance
applaud
application
approach
aptitude
archeology
archery
architect
argument
article
ashes
assistance
assistants
atmospheric
attendant
audible
aunt
authentic
autograph
awkward
axle
bankrupt
barricade
beautician
beautiful
because
beliefs
believe
bicentennial
bilingual
binocular
biography
biology
biopsy
biosphere
bipedal
bleachers
blind
blurted
borough
boundaries
boycott
brainstorm
briefly
brilliant
broach
brochure
brooch
brought
buoyancy
bureaucracy
burrow
buyer
campaign
careful
cartographer
castle
catcher
cautious
cease
censor
centennial
centipede
century
ceremony
chalkboard
championship
changeable
cheerful
chieftain
child's play
chorale
circuit
circumference
circumvent
citizenship
cleaner
cleanest
closure
collision
colonel
colorless
commented
compatible
concluded
condemn
confident
congenial
constitutional
conversation
coordinates
corduroy
corral
coughing
country
courage
courageous
courteous
courtesy
creature
credible
curious
customary
daughter
daybreak
decipher
delicious
demanded
describe
development
dictionary
disagree
discourage
disgrace
dishonest
distinct
does
doorknob
dormant
doubt
doubtful
drought
duffel bag
durable
eagerly
earnestly
earthworm
easel
echoes
effect
efficiency
efficient
effortless
electricity
embarrass
enact
encyclopedias
energetic
energy
enjoyment
enough
entry
envelope
environment
equality
equivalent
eruption
especially
establish
estimation
everybody
exaggerate
exclaimed
exhaustion
experiment
explained
export
expression
famous
fasten
favorite
feature
finally
finely
fixture
flexible
fluorescent
formal
formula
fracture
fragile
freighter
frequent
friction
friendlier
friendliest
friendship
frighten
fugitive
genuine
geography
geologist
geology
gestured
gesturing
glacier
glimpse
gnarled
goalie
government
grammar
graphite
grateful
grievances
halves
headquarters
hemisphere
hesitated
hesitating
high school
hockey
honorable
hooray
hostel
hostile
humor
humorless
humorous
ignorant
illegal
imitation
immature
immediate
immediately
immigrant
immobile
immortal
impatient
imperfect
import
inability
inanimate
incautious
incident
incite
inconvenient
indelible
independent
inertia
infectious
inquired
inquisitive
insight
insignia
insisted
instant
instruments
international
interrupt

journeys
judgment
knowledge
lecturer
leisure
lengthen
lithe
lonelier
loneliest
long-distance
loose
lose
lovable
loyalty
luxury
magazine
magician
magnificent
mayor
meager
meanwhile
membership
mentioned
menu
microscope
miniature
misbehave
misdirect
misfortune
misspell
moisture
molecule
moment
mosquitoes
museum
musician
national
natural
neither
nominee
nonconformist
nonexistent
nonfiction
nonsense
numerous
obedient
obey
obnoxious
observation
observed
obsolete
obstacle
obstinate
occasion
occurrence
ocean
officer
official
often
oily
ointment
old-fashioned
once
opinion
opportunity
opposite
optimistic
orchestras
ordinary
outstanding
ownership
oxygen
painless
pamphlet
parallelogram
participant
partnership
passersby
pathetic
patience
patients
patriotism
peninsula
perfectly
permanently
permission
perpendicular
persistent
persuade
persuasion
pharmacies
photograph
physical
physician
picturesque
pique
pitcher
plague
plausible
pleasant
pleasure
pliable
plight
plumber
pneumonia
poem
poetry
polyhedron
portable
powerless
preacher
precious
predictable
prediction
prescribed
prescribing
principal
principle
profitable
proverb
punctual
puncture
quietly
radiant
react
reaction
reappear
recede
received
recommend
referee
reformat
rehearse
reign
rein
reliable
reluctant
remarked
replied
respect
restrain
rewrite
rhombus
ridiculous
rupture
scented
schedules
scientific
screamed
sculpture
seize
seizure
semiannual
semicircle
semicolon
sensible
sensor
separation
sergeants
shipwreck
shortage
sighed
signal
signature
significant
similar
sincerely
skied
skiing
slight
solution
sparse
spectacle
spectator
starvation
stationary
stationery
stethoscope
stomachache
stowaway
straight
strengthen
studied
studying
stupendous
substances
successful
succession
sufficient
suffocate
sulfur
surely
survey
suspect
sweatshirt
symmetry
symphony
tedious
telescope
temporarily
terrain
their
themselves
theorem
they're
thieves
thorough
thoughtful
through
thumbprint
tireless
tomatoes
traitor
transact
transform
transport
trestle
triad
triathlon
triceps
triplicate
trolley
truancy
turmoil
twice
typhoid
typhoon
uncertain
underage
undercover
underestimate
underneath
unicorn
uniform
unify
union
unique
unit
universe
unlikely
unreliable
unsure
unusual
utilize
vacancy
valiant
valuable
varieties
vicious
videotape
vigilant
violation
voyager
waist
warning
wasteful
whined
whispered
wholesome
worthy
wrestling
xylophone
zealous

You are a SUPER SPELLER!

Name

Congratulations!!

Note: Corresponding Student Practice Book pages are indicated in parentheses.

Answer Key

Page 21 *(Page 5)*

Across	Down
1. restrain	2. anticipate
3. freighter	3. fragile
4. mayor	5. acre
7. straight	6. aptitude
8. obey	7. survey
10. agent	9. waist
11. persuade	10. axle

Page 22 *(Page 6)*

waist	obey
plague	restrain
straight	campaign
freighter	persuade
agent	survey
acre	anticipate
mayor	famous

1. waist
2. straight
3. freighter
4. persuade

1. fra	vey	1. fragile
2. fa	gent	2. famous
3. sur	bey	3. survey
4. cam	mous	4. campaign
5. re	cre	5. restrain
6. o	gile	6. obey
7. a	paign	7. agent
8. a	strain	8. acre

Page 23 *(Page 7)*

These words should be circled:

1. aunt	7. plague
2. survey	8. aptitude
3. axle	9. fragile
4. famous	10. acre
5. persuade	11. obey
6. campaign	12. anticipate

These words should be circled and written correctly:

1. persuade, aunt, campaign
2. famous, mayor, obey
3. agent, survey, acre
4. fragile, straight, waist

Page 25 *(Page 9)*

1. referee, hockey, illegal
2. Neither, believe
3. received, achievement
4. eagerly, easel
5. frequent, electricity
6. nominee, equality

Page 26 *(Page 10)*

1. illegal	10. achievement
2. neither	11. tedious
3. referee	12. entry
4. easel	13. hockey
5. pleasant	14. equality
6. abbreviate	15. nominee
7. received	16. electricity
8. frequent	17. eagerly
9. believe	

Rhymes with **week**—pique

1. 2	4. 3	7. 2
2. 4	5. 4	8. 3
3. 3	6. 2	9. 5

Page 27 *(Page 11)*

These words should be circled:

1. received	7. hockey
2. tedious	8. electricity
3. illegal	9. neither
4. believe	10. abbreviate
5. eagerly	11. achievement
6. frequent	12. easel

1. received, frequent
2. referee, pleasant
3. tedious, easel
4. nominee, eagerly, electricity

Page 29 *(Page 13)*

1. officer, obstacle, stowaway
2. poem or proverb, ceremony, envelope
3. Although, goalie, moment
4. often, proverb or poem
5. trolley
6. obstinate, antelope

Page 30 *(Page 14)*

long **o**	short **o**
although	molecule
poem	obstacle
moment	trolley
goalie	proverb
ceremony	oxygen
approach	obstinate
poetry	
stowaway	
envelope	
antelope	

1. 3	5. 2	9. 3
2. 2	6. 3	10. 3
3. 3	7. 4	11. 2
4. 2	8. 3	12. 2

Page 31 *(Page 15)*

These words should be circled:

1. envelope	7. obstinate
2. officer	8. approach
3. poetry	9. often
4. although	10. moment
5. ceremony	11. obstacle
6. oxygen	12. molecule

These words should be circled and written correctly:

1. officer, oxygen, goalie
2. ceremony, moment
3. although, stowaway, poem
4. approach, antelope

Page 33 *(Page 17)*

Down	Across
1. quietly	3. plight
2. friction	5. instant
4. distinct	8. scientific
6. typhoon	9. twice
7. describe	11. blind
10. glimpse	12. decipher
13. slight	14. pliable
	15. lithe

Page 34 *(Page 18)*

plight	twice	decipher
slight	describe	typhoon
lithe	blind	xylophone
buyer	pliable	quietly

1. in stant	7. ty phoon
2. buy er	8. pli a ble
3. dis tinct	9. qui et ly
4. fric tion	10. sci en tif ic
5. ac quire	11. xy lo phone
6. de scribe	

Page 35 *(Page 19)*

These words should be circled:

1. instant	7. xylophone
2. pliable	8. decipher
3. buyer	9. friction
4. twice	10. quietly
5. acquire	11. distinct
6. describe	12. scientific

These words should be circled and written correctly:

1. quietly, slight
2. instant, twice
3. buyer, acquire, scientific
4. describe, plight, typhoon

Page 37 *(Page 21)*

1. g
2. d
3. f
4. l
5. i
6. c
7. e
8. a
9. b
10. m
11. j
12. n
13. h
14. k

Page 38 *(Page 22)*

museum	universe	customary
does	menu	luxury
thumbprint	sulfur	unit
unusual	utilize	valuable
country	beautiful	fugitive

plural	add **s**	change **y** to **i**
1. countries		x
2. units	x	
3. fugitives	x	
4. sculptures	x	
5. thumbprints	x	
6. museums	x	
7. luxuries		x

Page 39 *(Page 23)*

These words should be circled:

1. luxury
2. suffocate
3. menu
4. utilize

These words should be circled and written correctly:
museum, valuable, sculpture, beautiful, once, country, does, customary, unusual, thumbprint, universe, fugitive

Page 41 *(Page 25)*

1. applaud, daughter
2. opportunity, terrain
3. recommend, exaggerate, because
4. brought, awkward
5. barricade
6. Hooray, authentic
7. symmetry

Page 42 *(Page 26)*

1. applaud
2. daughter
3. brought
4. awkward
5. because
6. authentic

1. opposite
2. occurrence
3. embarrass
4. opportunity
5. occasion
6. recommend
7. symmetry
8. exaggerate
9. barricade
10. terrain
11. alliance

1. 1
2. 5
3. 2
4. 3
5. 3
6. 4

Page 43 *(Page 27)*

These words should be circled:
symmetry, alliance, barricade, because

These words should be circled and written correctly:

1. awkward, terrain
2. opportunity, authentic
3. alliance, opposite
4. applaud, hooray
5. occasion, embarrass

Page 45 *(Page 29)*

1. cleanest
2. a. gestured
   b. studied
   c. hesitated
3. a. skied
   b. cleaner
4. loneliest
   friendliest
   cleanest
   angriest
5. skiing

Page 46 *(Page 30)*

add **ing**	no change	drop **e**
gesturing		x
hesitating		x
studying	x	
prescribing		x
skiing	x	

add **er**	no change	**y** to **i**
cleaner	x	
lonelier		x
friendlier		x
angrier		x

1. friendliest
2. gesturing
3. angrier
4. prescribed

Page 47 *(Page 31)*

1. gestured
2. angrier
3. loneliest
4. prescribing
5. hesitated
6. cleaner
7. friendlier
8. studied
9. skiing
10. cleanest

These words should be circled and written correctly:

1. studying, loneliest
2. hesitated, skied
3. friendliest, cleanest
4. angriest, gesturing, hesitating

Page 49 *(Page 33)*

1. g
2. h
3. l
4. k
5. j
6. m
7. d
8. e
9. b
10. i
11. c
12. f
13. a

Page 50 *(Page 34)*

1. everybody
2. anywhere
3. brainstorm
4. daybreak
5. high school
6. headquarters
7. themselves
8. meanwhile
9. stomachache
10. knowledge

1. videotape a e i o u
2. meanwhile a e i o u
3. daybreak a e i o u
4. high school a e i o u
5. absent-minded a e i o u
6. old-fashioned a e i o u
7. stomachache a e i o u
8. brainstorm a e i o u

Page 51 *(Page 35)*

These words should be circled:

1. everybody
2. duffel bag
3. brainstorm
4. outstanding
5. long-distance
6. sweatshirt
7. videotape
8. headquarters
9. absent-minded
10. old-fashioned

These words should be circled and written correctly:

1. daybreak, stomachache
2. anywhere, sweatshirt
3. everybody, themselves
4. headquarters, long-distance, brainstorm

Page 53 *(Page 37)*

Down
1. traitor
2. rehearse
3. circumvent
4. earnestly
5. favorite
7. courage
9. circuit

Across
4. energetic
6. courtesy
8. earthworm
10. similar
11. humorous
12. worthy

Page 54 *(Page 38)*

favorite traitor earthworm
worthy grammar courage
courtesy rehearse circuit
energy earnestly similar

Ways to spell **/ur/** = 6

1. trai — cuit
2. cir — worm
3. hu — age
4. wor — tor
5. earth — mor
6. cour — thy

1. traitor
2. circuit
3. humor
4. worthy
5. earthworm
6. courage

1. cou — vor — ly
2. earn — er — ite
3. cir — cum — gy
4. fa — ra — vent
5. en — est — geous

1. courageous
2. earnestly
3. circumvent
4. favorite
5. energy

Page 55 *(Page 39)*

These words should be circled and written correctly:
favorite, earthworm, traitor, energy, grammar, humorous, earnestly, similar, courageous, circuit, worthy, courteous

Page 57 *(Page 41)*

1. pleasure, bleachers, pitcher
2. archery, picturesque
3. puncture, fracture
4. lecturer, creature, natural
5. moisture
6. feature, fixture

Page 58 *(Page 42)*

1. feature
2. seizure
3. catcher
4. puncture
5. fracture
6. natural
7. archery
8. fixture
9. pitcher
10. leisure
11. closure
12. lecturer

1. preach er
2. mois ture
3. sei zure
4. bleach ers
5. pleas ure
6. frac ture
7. arch er y
8. pic tur esque
9. lec tur er
10. nat u ral

Page 59 *(Page 43)*

These words should be circled:
natural, feature, catcher, creature, closure, fixture

These words should be circled and written correctly:
1. preacher, archery, leisure
2. closure, picturesque
3. moisture, pitcher
4. creature, feature
5. lecturer, pleasure

Page 61 *(Page 45)*

1. typhoid
2. corduroy
3. amphibian
4. a. briefly
   b. flexible
   c. turmoil
5. ointment
6. pamphlet
7. symphony
8. boycott
9. loyalty

Page 62 *(Page 46)*

1. loyalty
2. oily
3. corduroy
4. typhoid
5. boycott
6. voyager
7. ointment
8. turmoil

1. physical
2. chieftain
3. flexible
4. symphony
5. amphibian
6. enough
7. pamphlet
8. coughing

1. enough
2. loyalty
3. ointment
4. oily
5. voyager
6. turmoil
7. flexible
8. efficient
9. chieftain
10. briefly

Page 63 *(Page 47)*

These words should be circled:
1. oily
2. voyager
3. enough
4. symphony
5. physical
6. ointment
7. coughing
8. chieftain
9. amphibian
10. efficient
11. flexible
12. loyalty

These words should be circled and written correctly:
1. amphibian, flexible
2. coughing, symphony
3. corduroy, oily
4. voyager, enough, physical

Page 65 *(Page 49)*

1. a. scented
   b. condemn
   c. doubt
   d. acknowledge
2. Any three of these words: doorknob, chalkboard, shipwreck, wholesome, honorable
3. a. honorable
   b. exhaustion
   c. gnarled
   d. wholesome
4. a. pneumonia
   b. sighed
   c. wrestling
   d. drought
   e. castle
   f. trestle

Page 66 *(Page 50)*

1. plumber
2. sighed
3. scented
4. shipwrecked
5. condemn
6. castle
7. gnarled
8. pneumonia
9. doubt
10. doorknob
11. wholesome
12. honorable

1. chalkboard
2. trestle
3. drought
4. condemn
5. acknowledge
6. exhaustion
7. wrestling
8. doorknob

1. plumber or doubt
2. doorknob
3. chalkboard
4. honorable

Page 67 *(Page 51)*

These words should be circled and written correctly:
exhaustion, sighed, doubt, gnarled, wrestling, shipwreck, condemn, scented, wholesome, pneumonia, castle, acknowledge, honorable

Page 69 *(Page 53)*

Down
1. colonel
2. shortage
4. opinion
6. magazine
8. warning
11. antenna
12. orchestra
14. algebra

Across
3. formula
5. efficiency
7. national
9. argument
10. ordinary
13. architect
15. appearance
16. participant

Page 70 *(Page 54)*

1. algebra
2. participant
3. orchestra
4. argument
5. architect
6. absolutely
7. opinion
8. magazine
9. national
10. formula
11. appearance
12. shortage

2 syllables

colonel warning shortage

3 syllables

national formula article
appearance argument magazine
opinion architect

4 syllables

ordinary participant
absolutely efficiency

Page 71 *(Page 55)*

1. article, national, magazine
2. opinion, orchestra
3. formula, algebra
4. colonel, absolutely, appearance
5. architect, shortage
6. antenna, ordinary
7. warning, argument

Page 73 *(Page 57)*

1. They're, their
2. assistants, brooch
3. sensor, burrow
4. borough
5. assistance, corral
6. reign, censor
7. broach, incite

Page 74 *(Page 58)*

long **a**	long **o**	long **i**
rein reign	brooch broach burrow borough	insight incite

1. in sight
2. cen sor
3. cho rale
4. bur row
5. sen sor
6. in cite
7. cor ral
8. bor ough
9. as sist ance
10. al read y
11. as sist ants

Page 75 *(Page 59)*

These words should be circled:
broach, chorale, censor, borough, assistance, they're

These words should be circled and written correctly:

1. They're, incite
2. already, corral
3. assistance, insight
4. their, brooch, sensor

Page 77 *(Page 61)*

1. c
2. f
3. j
4. k
5. o
6. l
7. h
8. n
9. i
10. b
11. d
12. m
13. e
14. a
15. g

Page 78 *(Page 62)*

1. expression
2. imitation
3. prediction
4. violation
5. estimation
6. separation

1. ac tion
2. am bi tion
3. mu si cian
4. beau ti cian
5. suc ces sion
6. star va tion
7. sep a ra tion
8. vi o la tion
9. ap pli ca tion
10. ob ser va tion

Page 79 *(Page 63)*

These words should be circled:
ambition, solution, violation, estimation, reaction

These words should be circled and written correctly:

1. persuasion, musician
2. reaction, starvation
3. application, beautician, solution
4. collision, expression
5. ambition, estimation

Page 81 *(Page 65)*

1. patients, principal
2. stationery, stationary, hostel, hostile
3. a. seize
   b. finely
   c. lose
   d. thorough
4. a. stationery
   b. hostel
   c. principle
   d. cease
   e. affect

Page 82 *(Page 66)*

1. lose, loose
2. finally, finely
3. hostel, hostile
4. patience, patients
5. cease, seize
6. principal, principle
7. through, thorough
8. effect, affect

Page 83 *(Page 67)*

These words should be circled and written correctly:
principal, through, stationery, effect, seize, hostel, finally, thorough, cease, patience, lose, affect, hostile

Page 85 *(Page 69)*

Across

1. brilliant
3. radiant
7. confident
9. immigrant
10. valiant
11. dormant
12. magnificent
13. vigilant
14. attendant

Down

2. ignorant
4. persistent
5. equivalent
6. significant
8. accident

Page 86 *(Page 70)*

1. per	luc	rant	1. persistent
2. con	mi	dant	2. confident
3. fluo	ci	lant	3. fluorescent
4. in	res	ent	4. incident
5. ig	sist	cent	5. ignorant
6. re	no	tant	6. reluctant
7. ac	ci	dent	7. accident
8. at	di	dent	8. attendant
9. vig	ten	grant	9. vigilant
10. im	fi	dent	10. immigrant
11. ra	i	ant	11. radiant

1. o	quiv	i	cent	1. obedient
2. sig	be	di	lent	2. significant
3. e	nif	i	ent	3. equivalent
4. mag	nif	a	cant	4. magnificent

Page 87 *(Page 71)*

These words should be circled:
confident, brilliant, radiant, immigrant, persistent, significant

These words should be circled and written correctly:

1. immigrant, persistent
2. radiant, brilliant
3. vigilant, attendant, reluctant
4. accident, ignorant

Page 89 *(Page 73)*

1. conversation, physician, sufficient
2. delicious, ocean
3. ashes, impatient
4. magician, ambitious, establish
5. Surely, brochure
6. permission, conversation

Page 90 *(Page 74)*

1. permission
2. establish
3. inertia
4. brochure
5. dictionary
6. magician
7. ocean
8. surely

Ways to spell /**sh**/ = 7

1. delicious
2. establish
3. impatient
4. official
5. ocean
6. brochure
7. permission
8. magician
9. ambitious
10. conversation
11. glacier
12. inertia
13. sufficient
14. physician
15. dictionary
16. friendship

Page 91 *(Page 75)*

These words should be circled:

1. friendship
2. ambitious
3. official
4. glacier
5. magician
6. impatient
7. surely
8. establish
9. ocean
10. conversation
11. delicious
12. brochure

These words should be circled and written correctly:

1. conversation, friendship
2. magician, permission, physician
3. glacier, ocean

Page 93 *(Page 77)*

1. b
2. g
3. l
4. k
5. j
6. i
7. e
8. d
9. c
10. f
11. h
12. a

Page 94 *(Page 78)*

1. indelible
2. sensible
3. predictable
4. audible
5. lovable
6. plausible
7. acceptable
8. compatible
9. profitable
10. durable

1. cau tious
2. cu ri ous
3. nu mer ous
4. au di ble
5. cred i ble
6. in fec tious
7. sen si ble
8. com pat i ble
9. pre dict a ble
10. prof it a ble

Page 95 *(Page 79)*

These words should be circled:
precious, numerous, infectious, audible, lovable, curious, credible

These words should be circled and written correctly:

1. curious, profitable
2. sensible, durable
3. cautious, precious
4. numerous, indelible

Page 97 *(Page 81)*

Across

1. beliefs
3. mosquitoes
5. grievances
6. tomatoes
8. boundaries
10. echoes
13. varieties
14. instruments
15. journeys

Down

2. schedules
4. encyclopedias
7. pharmacies
9. substances
11. passersby
12. halves

Page 98 *(Page 82)*

plural	**s** or **es**	**y** to **i**	**f** to **v**
1. halves			x
2. orchestras	x		
3. instruments	x		
4. varieties		x	
5. thieves			x
6. sergeants	x		
7. boundaries		x	
8. pharmacies		x	
9. echoes	x		
10. journeys	x		
11. substances	x		
12. tomatoes	x		
13. beliefs	x		
14. mosquitoes	x		
15. encyclopedias	x		
16. schedules	x		
17. grievances	x		

Page 99 *(Page 83)*

1. orchestras
2. pharmacies
3. encyclopedias
4. instruments, boundaries
5. journeys, mosquitoes
6. grievances, schedules
7. passersby, beliefs
8. thieves, varieties, tomatoes

Page 101 *(Page 85)*

1. a. powerless
   b. colorless
   c. humorless
   d. tireless
   e. painless
2. a. doubtful
   b. cheerful
3. e
   g
   a
   c
   f
   b
   d

Page 102 *(Page 86)*

1. painless
2. amazement
3. judgment
4. thoughtful
5. effortless
6. development

1. gov ern ment
2. suc cess ful
3. hu mor less
4. en joy ment
5. ef fort less
6. a maze ment

Page 103 *(Page 87)*

These words should be circled:
grateful, judgment, enjoyment, experiment, colorless

These words should be circled and written correctly:

1. experiment, government
2. colorless, cheerful
3. doubtful, successful
4. grateful, careful, effortless

Page 105 *(Page 89)*
1. unreliable
2. unlikely, immediate
3. immobile, independent
4. underestimate, immature or underage
5. inability, inanimate
6. imperfect
7. incautious
8. uncertain, undercover

Page 106 *(Page 90)*
1. unlikely
2. incautious
3. inconvenient
4. immortal
5. immobile
6. unsure
7. immature
8. unreliable
9. independent
10. inability

1. incautious
2. underneath
3. inconvenient
4. underestimate
5. immediate
6. unreliable
7. imperfect
8. immature
9. inability
10. uncertain
11. unsure
12. immobile
13. immortal
14. inanimate

Page 107 *(Page 91)*
These words should be circled: inability, inconvenient, uncertain, immature, unsure

These words should be circled and written correctly:
1. unlikely, unreliable
2. uncertain, undercover
3. unsure, underneath
4. underestimate
5. immature, independent, incautious

Page 109 *(Page 93)*
1. actor, autograph, photograph
2. geology, geologist
3. export, import
4. Geography
5. transport, graphite
6. biology
7. biography

Page 110 *(Page 94)*
1. act + or = actor
2. trans + port = transport
3. bio + graph + y = biography
4. geo + graph + y = geography
5. bio + ology = biology
6. im + port = import
7. geo + ology + ist = geologist

Page 111 *(Page 95)*
These words should be circled:
1. transact
2. autograph
3. geology
4. biosphere
5. transport
6. geography
7. graphite
8. photograph
9. biopsy
10. biography
11. enact
12. actor
13. import
14. portable
15. export
16. biology

Page 113 *(Page 97)*
1. admitted
2. whined
3. screamed
4. blurted
5. answered
6. demanded
7. explained
8. whispered
9. insisted
10. advised
11. mentioned

Page 114 *(Page 98)*
1. admitted—double last consonant
2. demanded—no change
3. replied—change **y** to **i**
4. whined—drop silent **e**
5. insisted—no change
6. advised—drop silent **e**
7. observed—drop silent **e**
8. screamed—no change

1. 2
2. 1
3. 2
4. 3
5. 2
6. 1
7. 2
8. 3
9. 2
10. 3
11. 2
12. 2
13. 2
14. 2
15. 3
16. 2

Page 115 *(Page 99)*
These words should be circled and written correctly:
inquired, replied, whined, screamed, mentioned, insisted, exclaimed, explained, remarked, demanded, observed, commented, admitted, whispered, concluded

Page 117 *(Page 101)*

Across
1. temporarily
5. permanently
7. buoyancy
9. strengthen
11. frighten
13. lengthen
14. citizenship

Down
2. especially
3. partnership
4. truancy
6. immediately
8. ownership
10. perfectly
11. fasten

Page 118 *(Page 102)*
1. immediately
2. permanently
3. temporarily
4. truancy
5. vacancy
6. buoyancy

7. citizenship
8. championship
9. ownership
10. lengthen
11. strengthen
12. frighten

1. sincere
2. length
3. member
4. permanent
5. vacant
6. partner
7. fright
8. buoyant
9. truant
10. temporary
11. perfect

Page 119 *(Page 103)*
These words should be circled: membership, ownership, buoyancy, truancy, immediately

These words should be circled and written correctly:
1. sincerely, citizenship
2. especially, perfectly
3. vacancy, immediately
4. membership, strengthen, championship

Page 121 *(Page 105)*
1. a. nonconformist
   b. nonfiction
   c. misspell
   d. antisocial
   e. misfortune
   f. recede
2. a. not
   b. again
   c. not
   d. not

Page 122 *(Page 106)*
1. nonsense
2. rewrite
3. dishonest
4. disagree
5. antiseptic
6. disgrace
7. discourage

1. misspell
2. nonfiction
3. disappear
4. indirect

Page 123 *(Page 107)*
These words should be circled:
misfortune, nonexistent, disgrace, discourage, recede

These words should be circled and written correctly:
1. antifreeze
2. misbehave, disgrace
3. nonexistent, disagree
4. nonconformist, dishonest
5. misfortune, misspell, antiseptic

Page 125 *(Page 109)*

1. abundant	8. inquisitive
2. ancient	9. stupendous
3. reliable	10. congenial
4. ridiculous	11. obnoxious
5. genuine	12. pathetic
6. punctual	13. optimistic
7. miniature	14. obsolete

Page 126 *(Page 110)*

1. optimistic	8. zealous
2. genuine	9. wasteful
3. reliable	10. obsolete
4. inquisitive	11. punctual
5. pathetic	12. congenial
6. ridiculous	13. abundant
7. sparse	14. stupendous

1. ridiculous, obsolete
2. meager, wasteful
3. ancient, reliable
4. congenial, genuine

Page 127 *(Page 111)*
These words should be circled and written correctly:
stupendous, miniature, inquisitive, ancient, ridiculous, obnoxious, congenial, optimistic, genuine, pathetic, obsolete

Page 129 *(Page 113)*

1. g	7. c
2. f	8. l
3. i	9. e
4. j	10. a
5. h	11. b
6. k	12. d

Page 130 *(Page 114)*

half	one
semicircle	union
semicolon	unify
semiannual	unique
	unicorn

two	three
bilingual	triad
bipedal	triplicate
binocular	triathlon
bicentennial	triceps

one hundred
century
centipede
centennial

Page 131 *(Page 115)*
These words should be circled:

1. unify	6. bipedal
2. centipede	7. unicorn
3. semicircle	8. binocular
4. bilingual	9. triad
5. century	10. unique

These words should be circled and written correctly:
1. triathlon, bicentennial
2. unicorn, centipede
3. century, bilingual
4. triplicate, semicolon

Page 133 *(Page 117)*
1. signature
2. stethoscope, microscope
3. uniform
4. spectator, eruption
5. suspect, bankrupt
6. interrupt, telescope
7. transform
8. formal, spectacle

Page 134 *(Page 118)*
1. rupt + inter = interrupt
2. form + uni = uniform
3. scope + micro = microscope
4. trans + form = transform

1. 3	9. 2
2. 3	10. 3
3. 3	11. 3
4. 2	12. 2
5. 4	13. 3
6. 2	14. 3
7. 2	15. 2
8. 3	16. 3

Page 135 *(Page 119)*
These words should be circled:
uniform, spectacles, stethoscope, transform, interrupt, respect, suspected, microscope, ruptured

Page 137 *(Page 121)*
1. cartographer
2. parallelogram, rhombus
3. Antarctica, Southern Hemisphere
4. archeology
5. peninsula
6. circumference
7. international
8. environment

Page 138 *(Page 122)*

Mathematics	Geography
theorem	peninsula
rhombus	Antarctica
coordinates	hemisphere
perpendicular	

Government	Science
constitutional	environment
bureaucracy	atmospheric
patriotism	

Page 139 *(Page 123)*
These words should be circled:

international	parallelogram
Antarctica	atmospheric
polyhedron	perpendicular

These words should be circled and written correctly:
1. cartographer, circumference
2. environment, Antarctica
3. parallelogram, perpendicular
4. international, peninsula

Frequent, Focused Practice Keeps Skills Sharp!

Daily Math Practice

Award-Winning

Grade appropriate, educationally sound, and designed to support your math curriculum. Based on NCTM standards, *Daily Math Practice* addresses key learning objectives including computation, problem solving, reasoning, geometry, measurement, and much more. Answer key and scope and sequence chart included. 128 pages.

Teacher's Edition		Student Pack (5 Student Books)	
Grade 1	EMC 750 978-1-55799-741-8	Grade 1	EMC 6527 978-1-59673-109-7
Grade 2	EMC 751 978-1-55799-742-5	Grade 2	EMC 6528 978-1-59673-110-3
Grade 3	EMC 752 978-1-55799-743-2	Grade 3	EMC 6529 978-1-59673-111-0
Grade 4	EMC 753 978-1-55799-744-9	Grade 4	EMC 6530 978-1-59673-112-7
Grade 5	EMC 754 978-1-55799-745-6	Grade 5	EMC 6531 978-1-59673-113-4
Grade 6	EMC 755 978-1-55799-746-3	Grade 6	EMC 6532 978-1-59673-114-1

Daily Word Problems

Watch your students' problem-solving abilities expand exponentially as they experience the theme-based, real-world applications presented in each of the 36 weekly sections. Monday through Thursday contain a one- or two-step word problem; Friday's format is more extensive and requires multiple steps. All problems are grade-level specific, with concepts including addition, fractions, logic, algebra, and more! 112 pages.

Teacher's Edition		Student Pack (5 Student Books)	
Grade 1	EMC 3001 978-1-55799-813-2	Grade 1	EMC 6539 978-1-59673-115-8
Grade 2	EMC 3002 978-1-55799-814-9	Grade 2	EMC 6540 978-1-59673-116-5
Grade 3	EMC 3003 978-1-55799-815-6	Grade 3	EMC 6541 978-1-59673-117-2
Grade 4	EMC 3004 978-1-55799-816-3	Grade 4	EMC 6542 978-1-59673-118-9
Grade 5	EMC 3005 978-1-55799-817-0	Grade 5	EMC 6543 978-1-59673-119-6
Grade 6	EMC 3006 978-1-55799-818-7	Grade 6	EMC 6544 978-1-59673-120-2

NEW!

Daily Academic Vocabulary

Daily Academic Vocabulary, the newest addition to Evan-Moor's popular "Dailies" titles, is a supplemental vocabulary series for grades 2–6. This series features direct instruction of vocabulary, shown to be the most effective way to expand students' vocabulary. Both reproducible teacher's edition and student practice book formats are available.

Two Great Formats!

Reproducible Teacher's Edition

- Definitions and sample sentences for each week's words
- Ideas for how to introduce the words
- Instruction that builds on students' personal connection to the words
- 32 Transparencies that display each week's words, definitions, and sample sentences

Student Practice Books

- **Days 1–4** each week present three or four practice items that focus on using the words in a scholastic or personal context.
- **Day 5** is a review that features four multiple-choice items and an opened-ended writing activity that requires students to apply the words to their own experiences.
- **Four quarterly review weeks** give students additional practice on the words introduced in the prior eight weeks. Practice formats include cloze paragraphs, crosswords, and crack-the-code puzzles.

NEW!

Teacher's Edition		Student Pack (5 Student Books)	
Grade 2	EMC 2758 978-1-59673-201-8	Grade 2	EMC 6507 978-1-59673-208-7
Grade 3	EMC 2759 978-1-59673-202-5	Grade 3	EMC 6508 978-1-59673-209-4
Grade 4	EMC 2760 978-1-59673-203-2	Grade 4	EMC 6509 978-1-59673-210-0
Grade 5	EMC 2761 978-1-59673-204-9	Grade 5	EMC 6510 978-1-59673-211-7
Grade 6	EMC 2762 978-1-59673-205-6	Grade 6	EMC 6511 978-1-59673-212-4